Also by Jane E. Pollock

Classroom Instruction That Works: Research-Based
Strategies for Increasing Student Achievement
(with Robert J. Marzano and Debra J. Pickering)

Improving Student Learning One Student at a Time

Improving Student Learning One Principal at a Time
(with Sharon M. Ford)

Minding the Achievement Gap One Classroom at a Time
(with Sharon M. Ford and Margaret M. Black)

Jane E. Pollock
with **Susan Hensley**

THE i5 APPROACH

LESSON PLANNING THAT TEACHES THINKING AND FOSTERS INNOVATION

 Alexandria, Virginia USA

1703 N. Beauregard St. • Alexandria, VA 22311-1714 USA
Phone: 800-933-2723 or 703-578-9600 • Fax: 703-575-5400
Website: www.ascd.org • E-mail: member@ascd.org
Author guidelines: www.ascd.org/write

Deborah S. Delisle, *Executive Director*; Stefani Roth, *Publisher*; Genny Ostertag, *Director, Content Acquisitions Editor*; Julie Houtz, *Director, Book Editing & Production*; Katie Martin, *Editor*; Georgia Park, *Senior Graphic Designer*; Mike Kalyan, *Director, Production Services*; Valerie Younkin, *Production Designer*; Andrea Hoffman, *Senior Production Specialist*

PAPERBACK ISBN: 978-1-4166-2456-1   ASCD product #117030   n11/17

PDF E-BOOK ISBN: 978-1-4166-2458-5; see Books in Print for other formats.

Quantity discounts are available: e-mail programteam@ascd.org or call 800-933-2723, ext. 5773, or 703-575-5773. For desk copies, go to www.ascd.org/deskcopy.

Library of Congress Cataloging-in-Publication Data
Names: Pollock, Jane E., 1958- author. | Hensley, Susan, author.
Title: The i5 approach : lesson planning that teaches thinking and fosters innovation / Jane E. Pollock with Susan Hensley.
Description: Alexandria, Virginia : ASCD, 2018. | Includes bibliographical references and index.
Identifiers: LCCN 2017038837 (print) | LCCN 2017049845 (ebook) | ISBN 9781416624585 (PDF) | ISBN 9781416624561 (pbk.)
Subjects: LCSH: Critical thinking—Study and teaching. | Information literacy—Study and teaching. | Cognitive learning. | Educational technology—Psychological aspects.
Classification: LCC LB1590.3 (ebook) | LCC LB1590.3 .P657 2018 (print) | DDC 371.3028—dc23
LC record available at https://lccn.loc.gov/2017038837

27 26 25 24 23 22 21 20 19 18   1 2 3 4 5 6 7 8 9 10 11 12

THE i5 APPROACH

LESSON PLANNING THAT TEACHES THINKING AND FOSTERS INNOVATION

Preface

Veronica Armstrong, a high school biology teacher, called me on Skype to discuss the new unit plans she was drafting in order to reflect the revised sequence of science courses at her school. "Jane," she said, "before we start on planning, do you mind if we talk a bit about the online course I am taking?" The class was great, she told me. It was called "Using Technology in the Classroom." Veronica explained that the first part of the syllabus was dedicated to knowing about the state's commitment to provide 1:1 technology (one student, one device) in every classroom. Then the instructor showed lots of exciting apps for students to use on personal devices in addition to numerous software programs available to teachers.

Listening to Veronica, it was clear how much she genuinely enjoyed learning about the different ways to incorporate technology into her classes. Making podcasts, she laughed, was the real hit among the teachers. Veronica commented that she thought her students would like some of the programs and apps she'd seen, but she was concerned about whether the technology would really help them become critical and creative thinkers and learn the biology content more effectively. "Am I out of line to wonder if using devices in class really leads to better learning?" she asked.

The Conundrum

It is no secret, Veronica continued, that students don't always use personal devices in classrooms in the way teachers intend. Students might appear to be actively taking notes on a laptop or researching online, but anyone strolling behind them would be sure to catch that instant screen change—the universal signal of a student hoping to avoid being caught doing something unrelated to a lesson. "It was bad enough when students stopped paying attention *before* personal devices," Veronica noted. "But now, technology seems to encourage distraction! If they are distracted, it is a chore to get them thinking about science."

Veronica confessed a second concern about student engagement and learning. "Please do not think I am complaining, but making a podcast and incorporating apps into my lessons requires a lot of planning on my part," she said. "For all that preparation, the result should be gains in student achievement. Does research confirm that my teaching efforts to use and encourage students to use technology in the classroom improves learning?" She said she had asked this question in her course's online chat, but noted, "The instructors and other participants only responded by posting studies indicating that students, parents, and teachers all reported higher motivation and satisfaction with implementing technology; there was nothing about thinking and improving learning."

My conversations with teachers indicate the same. Students seem more motivated to work on assignments when they use technology, but this has not necessarily translated into increases in test scores or grades. Some surveys reveal, and some teachers report, that students find class more engaging when they can use personal devices or electronic notebooks (Cox, 2015). Parents seem to concur, saying that their children like class more when they use technology (National Association of Elementary School Principals, 2013). It makes perfect sense, since students and everyone else seem to use technology effortlessly in everyday life. But very few studies show that incorporating technology into lessons improves overall student achievement (Hattie, 2009).

In fact, it seems the opposite may be true. In an article in *Psychological Science*, Pam Mueller and Daniel Oppenheimer (2014) share that taking notes on a laptop is a bad idea if you want to remember the information later. Their research showed that people who wrote out their notes longhand learned more deeply and remembered information much longer than those who word processed their notes on a digital device. If research shows that longhand note taking increases knowledge retention and deepens understanding, should teachers encourage students to use electronic note-taking programs? How can we advocate for "going paperless" in schools if going paperless does not improve learning?

Nicolas Carr, a journalist and Pulitzer Prize finalist, wrote about the quandary of digital vs. print in *The Shallows: What the Internet Is Doing to Our Brains* (2011). The title of the book foreshadows what he found: the internet is making us forget. Carr recounts his personal quest to determine how using technology was affecting his output; ultimately, he concluded that he could not. The problem, he says, was that he forgot much of what he read online, meaning that he was not able to think about topics in depth—and forgetting information is an anathema to a journalist. Acknowledging the risk of becoming known as a modern-day Socrates, who allegedly renounced the alphabet and writing, Carr cautions that using technology may increase consumption, but it's not likely to improve production.

In schools today, we use technology to present material and increase engagement, but is the time and money invested in classroom technology worth what seem to be negligible gains in achievement? I was determined to find a way to ensure that in-class technology use would magnify gains in student learning, productivity, and thinking.

Using Technology

I began the way Nicolas Carr did—by addressing my own experience using technology.

Electronic devices give me access to an almost infinite amount of information and visual representations through pictures or video. I use a laptop or other device to read news, studies, and books online, and I often click on links to see pictures or videos to give meaning to what I am reading. Inevitably, I send an e-mail or text, and I often contact the recipient afterward to discuss the information I've sent. Without a doubt, technology improves my life by giving me immediate access to information, images, and interaction with others, and this capability is not trivial. Perhaps the key to effective teaching with technology involves teaching students to tap into those environments—information and image seeking and interaction—rather than choosing an app or a program for a task.

To clarify, here is a story from my teaching past. In the days before students had personal devices in the classroom, I assigned research tasks that sent students to the textbook, the encyclopedia, or other print material in the school library's limited collection. For example, in a unit on the Industrial Revolution, I might have directed students to read about the conditions of workers in garment factories, meatpacking factories, and coal mines. Although I intended for them to find information that would allow for thoughtful comparison of these different working environments, support reasoned conclusions about the lives of these workers, and inspire original perspectives on the economies of the age, what students usually produced were well-organized sets of the same, predictable observations and conclusions. What I now realize was that the three or four paragraphs in the textbook, the encyclopedia, and our school library's print collection didn't give my students enough information to do what I wanted them to do—engage in deep thinking to generate original ideas. The resources available to them left them with literally *not enough to think about*. What's more, the student products didn't give me the evidence I needed to evaluate their analytical abilities or assess deep learning. I was left to determine grades by focusing on criteria such as whether they met the project deadlines, the appearance of the material, and presentation style.

Today, students using technology could approach a task focused on researching working conditions during the Industrial Revolution very differently. With ready access to the internet, they could synthesize information from numerous sources, including diaries, charts of the ages of workers, and documentation of work injuries. Images, photographic stills and video interviews with descendants of those who worked in factories or mines would provide critical details and generate interest. The task could easily be expanded beyond two or three types of environments to many other workplaces, and students could use the wealth of information available to engage in analyses and draw a wide range of conclusions about the impact of industrialization on different geographic areas or population settlements. Let's take a moment here to appreciate how invaluable digital devices are for tasks that require research and information gathering, because they provide such a breadth of information and images to support and drive inquiry, questioning, and reflection.

For many of us, digital devices are synonymous with communication. As events happen around the world, we reach out to others to seek clarification, find new or more or expertly curated information, get feedback, and receive correction. Now think of how students working on the Industrial Revolution task might interact with one another by editing shared text files and using video chats or messaging to join in conversations among themselves or with outside experts.

As I engaged in this kind of reflection, the need for using technology to teach thinking in class started coming into focus. The way to plan lessons for using technology in the classroom had to include opportunities for students to learn how to effectively access information and images, and for students to engage in some form of interaction for correction and clarification.

Eureka!

In *The New Executive Brain: Frontal Lobes in a Complex World* (2009) cognitive neuroscientist Elkhonon Goldberg writes about the prefrontal cortex, the brain's control center. It's here that each of us combines the information that we take in through our senses, processes it with labels and language, factors in our past or current interactions and experiences with one another and the world—and turns this all into *meaning.* Goldberg describes human cognition as forward looking and gives a name to the process humans use to manipulate and transform current and past information into a model of something that does not yet exist—*thinking.*

Reading Goldberg was my *Eureka!* moment.

The frontal lobes of the human brain are designed to seek out and process sensory information to use to generate new ideas. Consider students' lives in the noisy (ears), odorous (nose), and highly stimulating (eyes, touch, taste) outside world, and then consider a classroom where students have been primarily relegated to listening (ears) and seeing (eyes). If using technology in the classroom could increase sensory data about any given topic by providing an expanded supply of information, images, and interaction, then students would more likely do what comes naturally to the brain: think to generate new ideas. We may not be able to provide the tasting and touching sense in schools, but brain studies show that brains can make amazing adaptations when there is a need to compensate (Doidge, 2007). When teachers design lessons that expand the range of sensory inputs available to students, they increase the odds that students will engage in critical and creative thinking— otherwise known as *inquiry.*

And there I had my criteria for using digital devices not only to support learning, but also to build stronger thinking. Within lessons, technology should be employed in ways that encourage students to access *information, images,* and *interaction* that will power *inquiry* and lead to the generation of new ideas—otherwise known as *innovation.* The i5 approach was born.

The i5 Approach

To recap, the concept of the i5 approach emerged from blending the expectation that students use technology in class with the neurological explanation that a person needs sensory information—literally, something to "think about"—before he or she can generate original ideas.

Today, we can move forward from schools where chalkboards and hornbooks provided the environment for only the three r's (reading, 'riting, and 'rithmetic) to the 21st century classroom where digital devices provide the learning environment for the five i's: information + images + interaction + inquiry = innovation.

The i5 approach is a powerful lens that any teacher, from primary to secondary school and beyond, can use when planning lessons. Ask yourself, when should students look up more *information*? How would an *image*, video, or audio component deepen a student's understanding of a topic? Would *interacting* or receiving ongoing feedback through shared documents or instant communication clarify, correct, or deepen understanding that students can use to make meaning?

The i5 approach was immediately compelling to me, but I realized that it could not be about technology alone; teaching the *inquiry* skills needs focused attention. Think of it this way: in a world where information is only a click away, teachers should help students acquire and develop the critical and creative thinking skills to transform information, images, and interaction through inquiry into *innovation*.

Back to the Future

Nearly every school mission statement and strategic plan promises to increase critical and creative thinking skills, and many teachers say they use Bloom's taxonomy when planning and delivering instruction. But it's fair to say that most teachers do not explicitly teach thinking skills. My next step in refining the i5 approach was to figure out the best way to teach the thinking skills.

Looking back to the 1980s, the concept of teaching thinking in schools came to the forefront in education. Professional development for teachers in the United States responded to the memorable *A Nation at Risk* report issued in 1983, which identified an urgent goal for U.S. educators. Schools had to change; teachers needed to teach students how to become critical and creative thinkers.

If you search online for thinking skills programs that germinated during this time, you will find de Bono's *CoRT Thinking* (1986), Richard Paul and Linda Elder's *Critical Thinking* (2014), Art Costa's *Developing Minds* (1985), and Dimensions of Learning, a framework that I coauthored with our team at McREL Laboratory (Marzano et al., 1997). Based on evidence that most teachers wanted to teach thinking but needed a curriculum to show them how to do it, the different programs offered steps for teaching critical and creative thinking. What was not obvious to us at the time was that students and teachers, who faced a paucity of information in print materials, literally lacked the information that merited using robust thinking or inquiry processes. Teachers sensed the problem, but in the print world of the 1980s, we did not see any easy solution.

Then, the standards movement of the 1990s happened. The standards that emerged might have expanded and deepened content knowledge in a manner that would have given students more to "think about" and fueled critical and creative thinking, but political agendas steered educators away from this. The energy and funding that went into developing standards for testing and testing for standards was a devastating distraction to educators.

Thirty years later, not all is lost; in fact, with the dramatic advance of technology since 2007 and the widespread popularity and greater affordability of smartphones and tablets, timing may be in our favor. Based on the current standards and the available online content, there is plenty for students to think about. Students can search broadly for information and images about topics, and interact with many others, but they still need explicit instruction on how to inquire: analyze and evaluate what they find. We can revisit the thinking skills program, update the skills based on current neurological research, and produce the steps for teachers to teach inquiry.

This is a good time to clarify that in this book, the phrase *inquiry skills* is used synonymously with *critical and creative thinking skills*. To inquire is to ask a question and seek information, but *inquiry* involves studying, scrutinizing, and exploring. Some programs use the word to describe any unit of study that includes gathering information about a topic to resolve a problem, clarify doubts, or increase understanding. As noted, with the i5 approach, we make the distinction that teachers need to provide students with explicit instruction for learning inquiry or thinking skills; we do not assume that students know how to apply the steps of thinking to new information they encounter in school.

Rather than encouraging teachers to have students use technology, we can encourage teachers to teach students critical and creative thinking skills, *and that requires technology use.*

In This Book

In this book, my colleague and contributing author Susan Hensley and I describe that process. We explain how to design lessons that thoughtfully incorporate the wealth of inputs and options that technology makes available in today's classrooms and how to explicitly teach critical and creative thinking in a way that makes students skilled and powerful thinkers and ready innovators.

Chapter 1 gives an overview of teaching thinking for innovation, drawing on the works of neuroscientists who write for public awareness and practical uses. V. S. Ramachandran (2011), author of *The Tell-Tale Brain*, writes, "Brain science has advanced at an astonishing pace over the last 15 years, lending fresh perspectives on—well, just about everything" (p. xii). Although Ramachandran is well-versed in the new research, he has not abandoned traditional approaches that get positive results. For example, he suggests that his amputee patients seeking therapy for phantom limb pain use a cardboard box and a mirror at home rather than endure trips to hospitals to wait to use high-tech machinery. Ramachandran's work was a reminder to me that many teachers work in schools that do not have the latest technology—schools where students might still learn in a shared computer lab or use low-cost netbooks. The i5 approach doesn't require state-of-the-art technology; it works in any classroom with whatever technology is available to help teach students to think.

Even in the 21st century, teaching begins with a lesson plan. Chapter 2 explains where to start using the i5 approach and suggests that it helps to have a lesson-planning schema designed particularly for this purpose. We make the case, then, for the research-based schema called GANAG, introduced in *Improving Student Learning One Teacher at a Time* (Pollock, 2007). The first step in the lesson prompts the teacher to decide whether to teach procedural knowledge or to pursue a declarative goal that requires thinking. When lessons structured with GANAG are enriched with the i5 approach, students are best positioned for critical and creative thinking.

Chapters 3, 4, 5, and 6 delve deeply into the inquiry skills, exploring the four categories of association, synthesis, analysis, and taking action. Although they draw upon *Dimensions of Learning* (Marzano et al., 1997), where my colleagues and I produced a taxonomy of thinking skills, I rebooted the material for today's teacher, updating the steps of these skills to align with what we have learned over the past 20 years of research into how people learn, and giving special attention to the last step: generating new ideas, or innovating. These chapters focus on the component steps or skills, how to teach them, and how to incorporate them into lessons. Susan, an executive director of curriculum and instruction in the Rogers (Ark.) public school system, contributed many examples and recommendations for teachers. Working side-by-side with teachers in her district, she creates and teaches many classroom lessons. In these chapters, we present examples of lessons that have been enriched with the i5 approach to empower students to use technology to develop higher-order thinking skills and engage in innovation. Note that all of the lessons we present in the book are real lessons. We are grateful to the teachers who have shared them, many of whom have allowed us to identify them by name.

In Chapter 7, we revisit the iconic Horace Smith, the high school English teacher from Ted Sizer's (1984) fictitious Franklin High School, who faced a tsunami of school reforms in the 1980s. What would Horace do in a classroom where students bring their own devices?

Would the seasoned veteran change his teaching? Would his students learn better? Teachers, principals, and superintendents note that despite providing resources and professional development, technology implementation often sputters and fails like many other initiatives. What does new research on forming habits tell us about how Horace could implement the i5 approach in today's classroom?

The appendix that closes the book presents a reference list of the thinking skills explored in Chapters 3 through 6. It can guide you through each of these skills' steps and help you with the process of "i5-ing" your own lessons.

The Streetlamp

Let's return to Veronica, the science teacher who is learning to incorporate technology and hoping the efforts will result in gains in student thinking and learning. Reflecting on her question about the research reminded me of a vignette that Stuart Firestein (2012) includes in his book *Ignorance: How It Drives Science*.

Firestein relays the story of a scientist searching for his lost car keys in the area under a bright streetlamp one night. A passing stranger offers to help, but their search is unsuccessful. Finally, the stranger asks the scientist if he is certain that he dropped his keys in the area directly under the light.

To the stranger's surprise, the scientist answers that no, he actually lost the keys in another spot, pointing to a dark area of the street. When the stranger asks why he is not searching for the keys over there, the scientist responds that the light is much better under the streetlamp.

The anecdote seems set up to have us judge the scientist as silly for not looking in the right place, but Firestein shares the story to inspire discovery and innovation. He proposes that scientists seek information in areas where they have ignorance, not knowledge, and always look in the place where there is a possibility of finding something new, something useful, and something good. Firestein notes that he does not view science with a capital "S" and does not follow a set of rules to churn out hard, cold facts; in fact, he writes, "Science is groping and probing, and poking, and some bumbling, and bungling… and it's somehow exhilarating" (p. 2).

Similarly, teachers like Veronica do not view teaching with a capital "T," nor do they obediently follow a set of lesson planning rules or believe their sole purpose in the classroom is to ensure students master standards and hard, cold facts. Teaching, like science, is probing, poking, bumbling, and bungling resources to prepare lessons. Teaching is discovering ways to teach every child in school to probe, poke, bumble, and bungle as well, learning deeply and learning to conjure new ideas for their own generation and the next.

Some schools implement technology initiatives by looking for keys in the dark place where they are sure they have knowledge. Those schools will move ahead with 1:1 mobile device programs and celebrate students' satisfaction related to the use of technology, even if the devices are used for repetitive, low-level tasks. Some schools will provide the tools but miss the goal of using technology to teach students to be critical and creative thinkers.

The i5 approach is what I discovered when I searched for my lost keys under the bright streetlamp. I hope that teachers who read this book will use technology in order to teach students how to access an almost infinite amount of *information, imagery,* and *interaction,* but also that they will explicitly teach *inquiry* skills so students can practice becoming proficient at *innovation.* Now *that* would be exhilarating.

JEP

Teaching Thinking

Henry Molaison, or "HM," became a celebrity in the field of neuroscience—not for what he knew, but for what he did not know. In 1953, a surgeon removed a part of Henry's brain, the hippocampi, in an effort to reduce the occurrence of debilitating seizures. When Henry, then 27 years old, awoke from surgery, he could eat, breathe, walk, and talk; he seemed recovered and no longer suffered seizures. Soon, however, it became obvious that Henry had only a few long-term memories, and he was able to remember new experiences for just a couple of minutes, at the most.

Until his death in 2008, HM lived in "permanent present tense," as Suzanne Corkin put it in her 2013 book of that name. HM's procedural memory (what he could "do") was intact, but he had lost the ability to encode, store, and retrieve declarative information (what he needed to "know"). Over the next few years, neuropsychologist Dr. Brenda Milner, would point to his case as proof that people process procedural and declarative knowledge differently. It turns out that the surgeon removed the part of the brain that processes declarative knowledge, so Henry lost the need to think.

Thinking Naturally and Thinking *Better*

Humans with intact and healthy brains think. We *need* to think. We must sort through the thousands of bits of information we take in from the world around us, anticipate multiple reactions that might occur in response to any number of events, plan and predict consequences, and evaluate our actions to make adjustments. In other words, our daily interactions require us to think.

Many of our biological processes are automatic and happen naturally, but many of our procedural capabilities are developed through effort and practice. For example, in life and in school, we can get better at speaking a language, playing an instrument, singing a song, or building a cabinet. Can we get better at thinking?

In *The Brain That Changes Itself* (2007), psychiatrist Norman Doidge says yes. He describes Michael Merzenich's research that focuses on helping people think better. For example, Doidge writes, Merzenich and his team have developed practical exercises to support what they call the executive functions of the frontal lobes, including, "focusing on goals, extracting themes from what we perceive, and making decisions. The exercises are also designed to help people categorize things, follow complex instructions, and strengthen associative memory, which helps put people, places, and things into context" (2007, p. 90). In summary, Doidge notes that Merzenich's research shows that we can teach people to think better, and Merzenich and others offer training and exercises to support the executive functions. The next question is, are these newly acquired understandings of how the brain works something we can apply in schools?

We say yes. With so much information, imagery, and interaction to process from the outside environment, thinking—inquiry—is something of a survival mechanism. If students can become better thinkers through practice, and research says they can, making this a goal for schooling is both logical and correct. In schools, teachers are familiar with "guided" and "independent" practice time for students, recognizing that it's a necessary component of instruction aimed at building proficiency with procedural curriculum goals. Teachers can teach students to use and practice thinking skills to make meaning of the declarative knowledge in the curriculum and use that knowledge to generate original ideas and products.

Inquiry skills are a keystone of the i5 approach, which identifies 12 processes that teachers can teach students to use to gain deeper understanding of declarative content knowledge and become better thinkers overall. We group these processes into four categories (see Figure 1.1):

- **Association**
  Compare: Describe how items are the same and different.
  Classify: Group items together based on shared traits.
  Make analogies: Identify a relationship or pattern between a known and an unknown situation.

- **Synthesis**
  Investigate: Explain the theme of a topic, including anything that is ambiguous or contradictory.
  Construct an argument: Make a claim supported by evidence and examples.

- **Analysis**
  Analyze perspectives: Consider multiple takes on an issue.
  Analyze systems: Know how the parts of a system impact the whole.
  Analyze reasoning for error: Recognize errors in thinking.

- **Taking Action**
  Solve: Navigate obstacles to find a good solution to a problem.
  Decide: Select from among seemingly equal choices.
  Test: Observe, hypothesize, experiment, and conclude.
  Create: Design products or processes to meet standards and serve specific ends.

Taken together, these skills can be described as *the skills of inquiry*, and they've become familiar parts of the curriculum over the past few decades. Chances are, the lessons taught in most classrooms already feature most or all the skills listed above, and students are expected to use each of these processes to varying degrees.

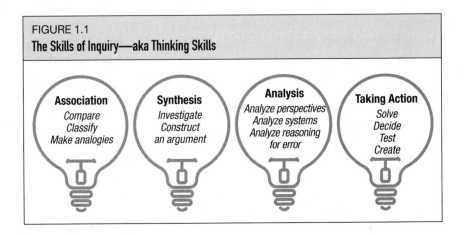

FIGURE 1.1
The Skills of Inquiry—aka Thinking Skills

But the critical question is whether teachers are deliberately teaching the skills of inquiry in the same way we might teach the steps of adding fractions, conjugating verbs, creating a website, making an omelet, or serving a volleyball? Do we teach students to compare, for example, or do we assign a task assuming they know how to compare? Do we expect students to be able to analyze points of view, or do we teach them to do this, step-by-step, and then give them the practice they need to get better doing it?

Following the i5 approach means ensuring that the lessons you deliver provide an opportunity for all students to learn to use inquiry skills to process all the declarative knowledge that we teach in school. And it means teaching, scaffolding, and reviewing these skills to help students become better, more innovative thinkers.

Two Types of Knowledge

This is a good place to clarify the confusion about declarative and procedural knowledge. These two types of knowledge are well-illuminated by David Bainbridge, the author of a book that looks at both the anatomy of the brain and the history of neuroscience, *Beyond the Zonules of Zinn: A Fantastic Journey Through Your Brain* (2008). Bainbridge explains that our brains process procedural and declarative knowledge differently. He describes how our ancestors spent a good amount of time seeking food as they moved through the rich natural environment, where they honed their abilities to see, hear, smell, taste, and touch. We have inherited brains that can move our bodies in productive ways. Exactly as our dogs and cats at home do, we use our cerebellum, or the "little brain," to move (and breathe, digest, circulate blood, etc.). These functions are automatic; *procedural knowledge* is the name we use for knowledge we have practiced enough times so that, once learned, its application *seems* automatic. With a bit of DNA and practice, some skills become automatic so that we can do them—*reproduce these actions*—without thinking.

Bainbridge continues his discussion about the need to procure food and inserts the idea that humans evolved beyond moving toward food (or away from it, in the case that they might become food to other animals) to remembering where food was stored, which food was in which area, and where it might be available again. Our ancestors generated a vast library of labels for this previously experienced information so that they could use it later and in new situations. This led to a much deeper demand than could be handled by just the "little brain." Our "bigger" brains grew to include a prefrontal cortex—an area of the brain that processes the type of knowledge known as *declarative knowledge*, or anything we know that we might "declare." Although the mechanism has not been pinpointed, we know that the evolution of language in humans coincides with the emergence of our prefrontal cortex. The human brains developed the ability to move our bodies but also to move ideas. The process for moving ideas needed a name to distinguish it from procedural knowledge, and it got one: *thinking*.

To become more proficient at skills—or procedural knowledge—a person practices. To productively use declarative knowledge, a person thinks. Thinking skills are the brain's way of processing declarative information for retention so that it can be manipulated and reorganized with other information to generate new ways to act.

The process of thinking is slow, and the thinker requires information and time to remember, reorganize, and produce results. In school, some tasks intend for students to reproduce knowledge (procedural goals), and other tasks intend for students to produce a new version of the knowledge (declarative goals).

Now let's identify insights about teaching thinking skills. A teacher can identify whether he or she wants students to learn a topic as procedural knowledge (to reproduce it) or as declarative knowledge (to retain and reorganize to produce an original insight). If the teacher decides to teach a topic procedurally, the students will need lots of practice and feedback. But if the teacher decides to teach information declaratively, then the students will need lots of information and an opportunity to learn and use the steps to one of the thinking skills.

Remember Bainbridge's description of hunters and gatherers moving through the rich environment and gathering input? Compared to the wilderness or a savannah, most classrooms come up short in terms of environmental stimuli; students generally hear and see, but there aren't that many opportunities to use the other senses of touching, tasting, and smelling the learning topic. That means that students need to compensate for the lack of stimulation to gather enough information, imagery, and interaction to set the thinking or inquiry processes in motion. The solution is to use digital devices.

Using technology compensates for the lack of stimulation in a print-only classroom. Complex sensory input is now more readily accessible than ever before, and students can view video and images, hear audio, and actively engage with what seems to be unlimited content and information. In short, the i5 approach informs the "why" of using technology in the classroom and directs digital devices into being a critical element of classroom instruction. It's a means to enrich the way students receive content and create the environment for developing better thinking.

As a side note, technology can be used in a way that improves students' procedural knowledge, too. Access to video, for example, allows students to watch a skill demonstration—and review it multiple times, studying each step as closely and as often as necessary. Access to video recording equipment in the classroom allows teachers and students to document skill development, to track progress, acquire feedback, and practice and perfect repetitive procedures. The caveat is that using technology can bolster procedural knowledge, but it cannot replace carrying out the procedure. You can read about swimming online, but most people agree that until you get in the water and start swimming, you will not become a better swimmer.

Technology deployed to develop declarative knowledge has fewer limitations. It gives students access to a seemingly unlimited amount of information to "think about" compared to what would be available in a non-digital classroom. Because our main concern in this book is the possibilities for teaching thinking that technology has opened we will be focusing on declarative knowledge and the thinking skills, leaving the discussion of using technology to improve procedural knowledge to another author.

How to "i5" Your Lessons

In the simplest application of the i5 approach, revising a current lesson is a matter of answering the "i5 questions":

1. How would more *information* help students see the details and breadth of this lesson's topic?
2. How would visual *images* or nonlinguistic representations add meaning to the topic or give it context?
3. How would *interacting* with others, live or through social media, provide clarifying, correcting, and useful feedback?
4. How would teaching or incorporating *inquiry*—a thinking skill—boost active engagement and questioning with the topic to increase aptitude?
5. What *innovative* ideas or insights could students produce in conjunction with this learning?

Let's take a closer look at each of these key questions and determine why they are so important before we move into lesson planning for teaching thinking and fostering innovation in Chapter 2.

The Role of Information

*How would more **information** help students see both the details and breadth of a topic?*

Just 20 years ago, a standard U.S. history textbook provided only one example of a constitution: the U.S. Constitution. Today, students can research information about "constitutions" online and find documents from dozens of countries in their native languages and translated into English. This breadth of content adds to students' understanding of nations and lays the groundwork for in-depth analysis using a higher-order thinking skill such as comparing different documents to find similarities and differences among them.

In *Think Better: An Innovator's Guide to Productive Thinking* (2008), Tom Hurson writes, "More than any other commodity, information is everywhere. Not only can almost anyone access almost anything at almost no cost, but, unlike corn and wheat, information doesn't have to be consumed to be used. Quite the opposite: the more it's used, the more it grows" (pp. 9–10).

In a classroom today, when Donna Martin teaches a poem by Gwendolyn Brooks or a novel by Gabriel García Márquez, her students have access to biographies, images of where and how these writers lived, critiques by both those who support and those who question their work, and, of course, recommended works shared by hundreds of people around the world. Ms. Martin says that when she is planning to deliver the new information in her lessons, digital sources are critical. She can direct students to visit websites to find biographical or autobiographical information; she teaches students to search for the right information they need to answer questions but also to delve deeper.

In Belinda Parini's physical education classes, students learn about factors that affect fatigue. Ms. Parini says she now plans instruction time to include short segments for students to search for information online.

By reading athletes' own writings, accessing data charts, and studying current science articles that support the knowledge of metabolic changes, students improve their abilities to predict fatigue factors and solutions in various case studies.

When planning to teach lessons today, many teachers search online to prepare their lectures or to present information to students. But teachers can also, and should also, have students use digital devices during class to search for information related to the learning goal and then teach them how to evaluate what they find for usefulness and accuracy. In the i5 approach, teachers and students access information during instruction to increase access to declarative knowledge, but also to become better thinkers.

The Role of Images

*How would visual **images** or video add meaning to the topic or give it context?*

Images are powerful. Henry Luce, the publisher of *Time* magazine, acquired *Life* magazine in 1936 so that readers could *see* the news, not just read about it. This new magazine literally changed the way its readers saw the world. A simple photograph of a young girl named Anne Frank gave a face to the Holocaust on the August 18, 1958, cover of *Life*. Similarly, the televised broadcast of the first step on the Moon's surface left an enduring footprint in viewers' memories.

Second grade teacher Lauren Eide enhances her students' comprehension in a social studies class as they learn about different cultures. They read *Four Feet, Two Sandals,* by Karen Lynn Williams and Khadra Mohammed (2007). Online, they see maps of areas to determine where the people in the book live and learn about challenges faced by residents of different geographic areas. They watch an online video about life in a refugee camp. The images and information support the reading, so that students discuss, question, and logically deduce what could happen in these parts of the world.

In *Classroom Instruction That Works* (Marzano, Pickering, & Pollock, 2001), Jane and her colleagues showed nonlinguistic representation as a technique with the high probability of improving student achievement, at $d = 0.75$. Stated differently, when students can see an image or a video of a person delivering an address in a theatrical production, hear sounds of animals, or see how chemical processes change substances through virtual experimentation, they attend to the content and remember it much better so they will store and use it again.

Some researchers say that 70 to 90 percent of the information that comes to the brain is visual. Because 40 percent of all nerve fibers connected to the brain are linked to the retina, the brain can process visual information 60,000 times faster than it processes text (Visual Teaching Alliance, n.d.). David Bainbridge (2008) suggests that when we discuss how humans process information, we should use "image" as a verb, not a noun; we *image* information as it comes to us, as our brains work to resolve the features of a new object or stimulus into a familiar picture so that we can respond to it more effectively.

When high school math teacher Becky Efurd teaches about parabolas, she shows a video of high jumpers in field competition as an illustration of an otherwise abstract concept. In health class, students can watch videos to find out how to tape a foot after an injury. Only a few years ago, students in Gary Nunnally's economics class learned about supply chains and the importance of coffee trade via a photo in the textbook, a few short paragraphs, and his lecture. Today, Mr. Nunnally plans lessons so his students can virtually visit a coffee plantation in Manizales, Colombia, where they are able to access information regarding the supply and markets. Students can view commodities trading online, in real time. They may not be able to smell the coffee via the internet, but they can access and experience information about the production and economy of coffee in engaging ways that encourage further research.

Using technology in the classroom, either by providing images or cuing students to search for an image, allows more students to more quickly engage in the topic of the lesson. Incorporating nonlinguistic representations in lessons provides opportunities for immediate engagement at any grade level and especially for students who speak another language at home. In much the same way that *Life* transformed

magazine reading, teachers using digital devices and the .
can transform classroom learning.

The Role of Interaction

*How would **interacting** with others, live and through social media, provide clarifying and useful feedback?*

As social beings, we crave interaction. Humans constantly seek, receive, and respond to feedback. Personal digital devices make such interaction in an educational setting a reality for students, thanks to the individualized and often immediate feedback they can provide. Websites and programs such as Google Hangouts, instant messaging, texting, Skype, Facetime, and even the more traditional e-mail exchanges are optimal tools for interaction. We are lucky to live in a time of instant communication.

As we consider how to encourage students to interact with others, however, we must address two challenges that are brought to our attention by neuroscience research. The first is that human brains developed to seek distractions. Because distractibility (for food sources) is a trait that helped our ancestors survive, it persists in the gene pool today. In the hands of children, digital devices offer zillions of personal distractions, so using technology in the classroom will usually trigger a positive reaction from students; they will like it.

The second challenge is that humans are natural socializers or, as David Bainbridge (2008) describes us, "compulsive communicators" (p. 307). Today all of us seem to use digital devices to feed our compulsion. Introduce a social media network to teenagers who are still amygdalating (OK, that's not a real word, but it implies emoting instead of reasoning) and lack fully-formed prefrontal cortices, and these students will be all but compelled to interact at the click of a keyboard or the swipe of a fingertip.

At this point, you might be thinking that interaction may not be such an advantage to learning in a classroom, but it can be highly productive. In the language arts classroom, students writing a story or a speech can receive immediate feedback if they share a file or work on a shared document. In world language classes, students can practice conversation via Skype links between Boston and Bucharest or Cedar Rapids and Caracas. In science, interaction in lab settings epitomizes the work of pairs of young scientists who use digital devices to make quick searches, check accuracy, and organize information.

The sobering aspect of distraction and socialization is that as much as we humans enjoy them, we are wired to set goals. In any situation, humans set goals and then strive to connect new information to previously experienced knowledge so we act, either quickly or in well-planned or strategically thoughtful ways, to meet those goals. To be specific, in a classroom setting the learning intention is critical. If it is clear to students at the onset of the lesson, the human need for interaction (pair-sharing, talking at tables, shoulder partners) can be used as a tool to encourage them to interact for clarification, correction, and to seek more information to meet the goal or objective for the lesson.

Feedback is necessary for effective learning and can come from multiple sources. The essence of interaction in the i5 approach is that students learn to seek input or correction from the teacher, from themselves by searching, and from others to clarify information or rectify mistakes. Obtaining feedback in a classroom often means frequent and timely interaction and students can use digital devices to focus and streamline these exchanges.

The Role of Inquiry

*How would teaching **inquiry** or a thinking skill boost active engagement and questioning with the topic to increase aptitude?*

The i5 approach for planning lessons supports teaching and developing students' thinking power. It's built on findings about the executive functions offered by the neuroscientists, research on effective instructional approaches that formed the basis of *Classroom Instruction That Works* (Marzano et al., 2001) and a series of thinking skills that Jane and these same colleagues developed in the book, *Dimensions of Learning* (Marzano et al., 1997). And although teaching thinking is compatible with various lesson planning approaches, it is best facilitated through a schema called the Master Learners model (GANAG) first published in *Improving Student Learning One Teacher at a Time* (Pollock, 2007). In *Classroom Instruction That Works*, Jane and her colleagues found that three areas of thinking showed high effect sizes: identifying similarities and differences ($d = 1.61$), generating and testing hypotheses ($d = 0.61$), and questioning ($d = 0.59$). The inquiry aspect of the i5 approach emerged from the research in those categories of thinking. The 12 thinking skills in Figure 1.1 are the focus of inquiry instruction.

Students come to class with the natural ability to think in the world around them; our challenge as teachers is to teach them to effectively think about math, humanities, music, and the other content we teach in school. The i5 approach guides teachers to do just that—and to enlist digital devices in the effort.

Fostering Innovation

*What **innovative** ideas or original presentations could students produce?*

Elkhonon Goldberg (2009) writes about how the prefrontal cortex powers the actions we take. Humans with healthy brains are constantly encoding, storing, and retrieving information in response to newly sensed information. Thinking is powered by memory. We can retrieve and apply that information to the various new tasks, decisions, situations, and interactions we face. And it's the frontal lobes we rely on to do that work.

According to Goldberg, what makes humans unique is that we can generate a mental picture of something that does not exist—like a mermaid, for instance. Before Disney animation, and even before libraries filled with illustrated volumes, people were calling up images of fish they had seen and combining it with the image of a human being to create the visual concept of a mermaid; this was thanks to the function of their prefrontal cortices. In short, the frontal lobe is used to produce original thoughts with newly sensed or remembered information. Humans use the prefrontal cortex to think so that they can innovate.

Economist Tom Grasty (2012), considering what skills will be beneficial within society in the years ahead, shares an interesting distinction between invention and innovation:

> In its purest sense, "invention" can be defined as the creation of a product or introduction of a process for the first time. "Innovation," on the other hand, occurs if someone improves on or makes a significant contribution to an existing product, process or service. (para. 5)

Grasty notes that after the invention of the transistor, most of the products we use today could arguably be considered "innovations," rather than inventions. Innovation, he believes, is what we need to be teaching students.

With access to digital devices and the internet, students can seek information or view images to add meaning to a topic, interact with others to seek feedback, and use all those memories to power their own ideas, through inquiry, to innovate.

The i5 Student and 21st Century Skills

Susan's son, Samuel, is a typical high school student. Technology use is part of his daily life. In addition to using the internet to download songs and videos for entertainment, he searches for information to help him learn the newest dance steps, refine his soccer moves, improve and record his trumpet practice, or find the instructions for assembling a new bookcase for his bedroom. He interacts with friends through texts and shares images through social media. Samuel games with friends he will never meet face-to-face.

Our professional challenge is to teach students like Samuel to apply 21st century skills to their academic lives as effortlessly as they apply them to their personal lives. There are several different interest groups with varying definitions of what students should know and be able to do in the 21st century. What exactly are the 21st century skills we want students to use?

The Partnership for 21st Century Learning (P21, formerly known as Partnership for 21st Century Skills) coalition has spent more than a decade bringing 21st century skills to the center of education in the United States and has developed a guiding framework (P21, n.d.). Bernie Trilling and Charles Fadel, authors of *21st Century Skills* (2009), narrow the list to three main categories: learning and innovation skills, digital literacy skills, and life and career skills.

The International Society for Technology Education (ISTE) produced the National Education Technology Standards for Students in 2009. The revised 2016 version describes indicators for seven standards, including Empowered Learner, Digital Citizen, Knowledge Constructor, Innovative Designer, Computational Thinker, Creative Communicator, and Global Collaborator.

What they have in common is that they both attempt to describe what students in the digital era need to know and be able to do to demonstrate knowledge and to use available tools to research, create, and communicate.

The i5 approach provides a way to teach students to meet these indicators in the classroom, and it helps produce citizens who will succeed in the increasingly digital world. If the P21 and ISTE/NETS standards describe what we want for our graduates, the i5 approach describes how to pursue it.

The Other "i"

To paraphrase Ralph Waldo Emerson, "Every artist began as an amateur." The intent of the i5 approach is to guide our amateur students to use digital resources to become their very best selves. Inspired by Emerson, the i5 approach encourages teachers to teach so that students learn to think for themselves, actively self-assess, and relentlessly seek and use resources available to become their very best. The goal for students using the i5 approach can be captured with another "i"—to be a contributing *individual*.

The i5 Plan for Instruction

Sir Francis Bacon (1561–1626) touted the scientific value of observation. He is said to have offered up this story, which he allegedly found in the records of some Franciscan friars:

> In the year of our Lord 1432, there arose a grievous quarrel among the brethren over the number of teeth in the mouth of a horse. For thirteen days, the disputation raged without ceasing. All the ancient books and chronicles were fetched out, and wonderful and ponderous erudition such as was never before heard of in this region was made manifest. At the beginning of the fourteenth day, a youthful friar of goodly bearing asked his learned superiors for permission to add a word, and straightway, to the wonderment of the disputants, whose deep wisdom he sore vexed, he beseeched them to unbend in a manner coarse and unheard-of and look in the open mouth of a horse and find answer to their questionings. At this, their dignity being grievously hurt, they waxed exceeding wroth; and, joining in a mighty uproar, they flew upon him and smote him, hip and thigh, and cast him out forthwith. For, said they, surely Satan hath tempted this bold neophyte to declare unholy and unheard-of ways of finding truth, contrary to all the teachings of the fathers. After many days more of grievous strife, the dove of peace sat on the assembly, and they as one man declaring the

problem to be an everlasting mystery because of a grievous dearth of historical and theological evidence thereof, so ordered the same writ down. (Simanek, 2014)

This parable is meant to humorously convince the reader that sometimes going right to the horse's mouth is the best way to proceed. We keep this in mind as we begin to discuss the i5 approach to use technology to teach thinking.

The next few pages are our very own interpretations of opening the horse's mouth and counting its teeth. We are going to look at how teachers plan and deliver lessons. Do the models they use explicitly teach inquiry or thinking? Do these models encourage using technology to increase access to information, images, and interaction so that students can think to generate new ideas? Of course, we are very aware that, to some audiences, the suggestion that we look at lesson planning in the 21st century is an awfully mundane task, so we are at risk of being flown upon and smote, hip and thigh!

Planning to Teach Thinking

Jonas Beck, who teaches in Arkansas, described his dilemma and asked some key questions:

> Next year, we must show that we teach critical and creative thinking *and* use technology in the classroom because students will have netbooks. I plan my lessons to cover the content. Sometimes lessons go longer than I expected, so we finish them the next day. Is it only social studies that spills over, or is there a way to plan my lessons so we get the job done? The way I learned to plan was at the unit level. I would begin with a list of learning activities to try to fit in, but I could never manage to do them all, much less add technology and thinking skills.
>
> Social studies, by definition, is thinking skills—it is thinking about the past, present, and future—so I don't see how I should plan any differently. Also, to be honest, when students have digital devices in class, I cannot get them to pay attention, so I mostly let

them use their devices when they finish the lesson activity. Sometimes I use Kahoot! [a game-based quizzing platform] or another program that lets me assess students in class, but I cannot do that every day if I am going to cover the content.

My question is, how do I show thinking skills and incorporate technology in my lesson plans? I am not sure how to write it down if one happens naturally and the other is something that I may or may not implement based on the students' behavior.

Mr. Beck represents many 21st century teachers. He plans lessons to address the content of his curriculum standards and then attempts to "add on" any new initiatives the school is pursuing. To him, "lesson planning" means fitting what he needs to cover into a limited amount of time. For teachers to successfully integrate initiatives like technology implementation or thinking skills instruction into their existing lesson planning and delivery, they need to know how to ensure that there will be sufficient time to do it. Teachers will have to look at the horse's mouth; they will have to examine their own lesson-planning habits before they can "i5" those lessons.

Let's backtrack a little. A useful term used to describe the integration of technology into classrooms is *blended learning*. The intention of blended learning is to use technology to make lessons more student-centered—more personalized—as students learn through online methods as well as face-to-face. Students wind up with more control over the place and pace of their learning. From a teacher's perspective, technology can be used as a mechanism for providing more individualized instruction. Blended learning often takes place according to a rotation model that alternates activities or assessments that are grounded in technology with offline instruction; alternatively, technology might be used to provide a portion or all of the instruction, as is the case with flipped classrooms or online courses.

Using technology to personalize instruction, monitor progress, and scaffold learning works, but can teachers boost learning further by finding ways to incorporate technology into common lesson planning to transform some low-level learning to higher-order, deep thinking? The i5 approach helps teachers determine when during the lesson students would benefit from the information, images, interaction, inquiry, and innovation that technology fuels. In other words, it provides the opportunity to teach students to use digital resources to do the following:

1. Search for *information.*
2. Use visual *images* and nonlinguistic representations to add meaning.
3. *Interact* with others, live or through social media, to obtain and provide feedback.
4. Use *inquiry* skills to deepen knowledge.
5. Generate *innovative* insights and products.

Mr. Beck said that he teaches from curriculum units but not daily lesson plans. The truth is, to use technology and teach thinking skills, one needs to zoom in to that daily-lesson level. Let's examine how most teachers plan daily lessons by considering three commonly used lesson planning models. Then we will see where and how the i5 approach fits.

The Mastery Teaching Model

Madeline C. Hunter (1994) positively revolutionized teaching, and her Mastery Teaching lesson planning model is probably the most commonly used tool in schools today. There are five basic steps to the model:

1. Set a learning objective.
2. Provide an anticipatory set to hook students' interest.
3. Teach with input and modeling.
   Check for understanding/monitor and adjust instruction as needed.
4. Provide students with guided practice.
   Check for understanding.
5. Provide students time for independent practice.
   Check for understanding.
* Provide closure (added to the schema later).

Preservice and first-year teachers tell us that their university instructors currently teach the Hunter method with two additional components: technology infusion and differentiation for students with special needs.

According to Hunter's research, when teachers in all subjects used this methodology for planning the delivery of instruction, they made a significant positive impact on student learning. As we begin to consider the i5 approach to using technology to teach thinking, it's worth asking two questions. First, where in the Hunter model are teachers currently using technology to help students meet the learning intentions of the lessons? Second, where are they explicitly teaching thinking skills and asking for thinking skill application? It is important to note at this point that the Hunter model explicitly identifies where to guide and provide *practice*.

The Workshop Model

In the early 1980s, Donald Graves (1983) transformed the teaching of writing, and his colleague, Lucy Calkins (1986) expanded this technique for reading instruction and called it the Workshop model. Many teachers use the Workshop model for writing and reading instruction because it allows for differentiation in addition to whole-group instruction. It directs teachers to establish a routine for each lesson:

1. Mini-lesson (20 percent of the lesson time)
2. Independent work time (60 percent of lesson time)
3. Share session (20 percent of the lesson time)

The teacher provides direct and explicit instruction to the whole class in the mini-lesson for 10 to 15 minutes, using a "think aloud" technique to model steps to meet the goal of the lesson (e.g., mastering a reading comprehension strategy or a writing technique). Students can then practice the skill as they read or write alone, in pairs, or in small groups during independent work time. The teacher confers with individuals and small groups during this time to informally assess their understanding of the lesson. The workshop session ends with a share session, during which the teacher highlights several students' work as it relates to the mini-lesson goal, recaps the learning, provides enrichment, and checks for understanding. The Workshop model has similarities to the popular Gradual Release of Responsibility model that transfers mastery of skills from the teacher to the student (Duke & Pearson, 2002; Pearson & Gallagher, 1983).

The Workshop and Gradual Release of Responsibility models were designed primarily for teaching literacy skills of reading and writing. Those skills are procedural knowledge, so the lesson schema encourages practice for students to reproduce the skills. Not surprisingly, many math classes also use a variation on these two models, streamlining the process to: *I do, we do, you do.*

Now we'll pause to ask the same two questions about the Workshop model that we did of the Hunter model: Where would an influx of technology improve the learning? Where would teaching and applying inquiry fit into the lesson?

The BSCS 5E Instructional Model

Just to explore a different type of model, let's take a few minutes to look at the BSCS (Biological Sciences Curriculum Study) 5E instructional model, which is inquiry-based and, thus, focuses on teaching declarative content knowledge. Based on work done by Karplus and Thier (1967) at the University of California at Berkeley for the 1967 Science Curriculum Improvement Study (SCIS) and further developed in late 1987 for science education, the 5E model approaches science as discovery by identifying five phases of student learning:

- Engagement—access students' prior knowledge and engage their interest in the content
- Exploration—introduce students to an activity that facilitates conceptual change
- Explanation—encourage students to generate an explanation of the phenomenon

- Elaboration—challenge students' understanding and provide new experiences to deepen their learning
- Evaluation—have students assess their understanding of the content (BSCS, 2016)

The 5E model restructures the typical direct instruction lesson by providing exploration time, or student independent work, at the beginning of the lesson. Students engage, ask questions, predict, and record observations. This method requires teachers to offer well-timed feedback and elaboration to deepen the learning. This schema seems to naturally allow time for "thinking," and it provides opportunity for the skill we refer to as the scientific method (and now we know there are other thinking skills) and eschews direct instruction of the thinking skill in favor of discovery learning. The 5E model is a good framework so long as the teacher realizes that he or she should explicitly teach the inquiry skills and use these skills to guide the discovery of lesson content; this step is implicit in actual classroom practices.

All the models for lesson planning we've looked at should continue to be used, but each is specific to a type of content instruction and does not provide an approach that can be used for *all* lesson planning. The next section makes a case for using a schema that allows for teaching procedural knowledge or declarative knowledge, so that students learn to practice or to use a thinking skill.

The Master Learners Model

In this section, we offer a lesson planning schema that cues teachers to identify whether they intend for the students to learn the daily lesson goal(s) as procedural knowledge (and practice) or declarative knowledge (and use an inquiry skill).

A quick reminder about the distinction between procedural and declarative knowledge: knowing how to fly an airplane is procedural knowledge and requires lots and lots of practice; knowing a lot about airplanes is declarative knowledge and one uses thinking skills to improve upon the existing design or generate new ideas about airplanes.

Although we do not typically dissociate procedural and declarative knowledge in everyday life, in the classroom it's advantageous to do so, simply because the two types of knowledge are applied through different instructional methods and different parts of the brain.

Procedural knowledge is best learned with modeling, guided practice, and independent practice. For that type of learning, we suggest using the Hunter model, Workshop, or Gradual Release as they were designed expressly for that reason. However, when the lesson goal calls for students "to know" more (acquire declarative knowledge), what's called for are instructional methods that help students organize and retain as much knowledge as possible. In 2007, Jane updated Madeline Hunter's Mastery Teaching schema for that very reason. In *Improving Student Learning One Teacher at a Time* (Pollock, 2007), she suggests that teachers can plan to teach either declarative or procedural knowledge using the same schema. She also renamed the schema calling it the Master Learners model because the result of using it is "master learners," not "master teachers." This model is also known as GANAG—a reference to the model's five steps:

> **G**oal—Set a goal of teaching declarative or procedural knowledge
> **A**ccess students' prior knowledge
> **N**ew Information—For declarative knowledge, teach the information plus the steps to an inquiry skill; for procedural knowledge, teach the steps for that procedure.
> **A**pplication—For declarative knowledge, have students apply the acquired information using a thinking skill(s); for procedural knowledge, have students practice the steps in new situations.
> **G**oal Review—Review the lesson goal and provide a way for students to self-assess.

Feedback (from teacher, peers, and self) between steps helps to further deepen student understanding.

The essence of GANAG is that it allows teachers to plan for students to learn the steps of procedural knowledge and practice these steps to increase performance, but, more importantly, it encourages *planning* for students to acquire information and use an inquiry or thinking skill in order to apply that declarative knowledge to make meaning, transforming knowledge from simple recall into new original ideas. Most teachers agree, and it is well-documented, that early elementary grades primarily teach reading, writing, and other skills, and emphasize procedural knowledge. At about grade 3 or 4, however, the curriculum flips—as the well-known phrase puts it, from "learning to read to reading to learn." This cataclysmic shift—from teaching mostly procedural knowledge to teaching mostly declarative knowledge, from "just practicing" to "practicing and thinking," calls for an updated lesson planning schema. What's more, the Workshop and Gradual Release models work well for reading and writing but not as well for teaching highly declarative social studies and science lessons. We make the case for GANAG because the other models, sometimes inadvertently and sometimes by design, fail to guide teachers to explicitly teach thinking when the content calls for it.

Teaching, according to Hunter's original model, leads to students "practicing" all knowledge rather than applying higher-order thinking skills to newly acquired declarative knowledge. Without intending to do so, teachers plan for students to practice declarative knowledge, and the result is simply memorizing for recall. In other words, it guides students to just learn content and not necessarily to *think* about it. Being that we are two of Hunter's greatest admirers, we hope that she would proudly embrace the update of her schema that applies the findings of neuroscientific research. We have no doubt that if Hunter were alive today, she would update her model to include research from the burgeoning field of neuroscience and revise her "Teach with input and modeling" step to a bifurcated option: *If teaching procedural knowledge, teach the steps and then practice; if teaching declarative knowledge, then teach and use a thinking skill.*

As we mentioned earlier, a teacher can incorporate technology when teaching procedural knowledge to show a procedure, give feedback, and guide practice, but our focus in this book is making the case for teaching critical and creative thinking by using technology. Let's return to the i5 approach. If you combine GANAG and the i5 approach, you increase the opportunity for students to use technology to gather new information (N) and use thinking skills in the application (A) to generate new insights. We'll look at that next.

Research-Based Lesson Planning

In addition to updating lesson models that were created before the routine use of fMRIs and other equipment used to study how the brain makes memories, GANAG also extends teaching and learning a bit further with research from a meta-analysis on powerful learning.

GANAG emphasizes student engagement and enhanced student learning because Jane designed it specifically to incorporate nine "high-yield strategies" (instructional techniques that have a positive effect size of higher than $d = 0.50$ in improving student achievement), which are introduced in the study she coauthored, *Classroom Instruction That Works* (Marzano et al., 2001). The nine high-yield strategies and their respective positive effect sizes are

- Identifying similarities and differences ($d = 1.61$)
- Summarizing and note taking ($d = 1.00$)
- Reinforcing effort and providing recognition ($d = 0.80$)
- Homework and practice ($d = 0.75$)
- Nonlinguistic representations ($d = 0.75$)
- Cooperative learning ($d = 0.73$)
- Setting objectives and providing feedback ($d = 0.61$)
- Generating and testing hypotheses ($d = 0.61$)
- Questions, cues, and advance organizers ($d = 0.59$)

Observing that professional development lacked explicit instruction on how teachers could incorporate these strategies into daily lessons, Jane designed GANAG to include examples of areas of fit for each of the nine strategies (see Figure 2.1). The updated GANAG is not just a modernization of Hunter's model or way to improve teaching; it is the way to improve student learning based on research studies.

FIGURE 2.1

The GANAG Lesson Plan Format That Includes High-Yield Strategies

Phase Description	High-Yield Strategies	Notes
G—The teacher sets the **goal** for the lesson based on grade-level standards (curriculum). The goal may be declarative or procedural. Students write the goal and self-assess both on their understanding and effort they will put into the lesson.	• Setting objective and providing feedback • Reinforcing effort and providing recognition	*In the Hunter model, the teacher states the goal and discusses it briefly, but does not intentionally teach students to write it down and self-assess their pre-lesson understanding and how much effort they would apply to learning that day.*
A—The teacher cues students with an image or nonlinguistic representation to fire neurons in **anticipation** of the topic of the lesson. Students write their responses and share with partners or tablemates.	• Nonlinguistic representations • Cooperative learning • Questions, cues, and advanced organizers	*In the Hunter model, the teacher may ask a question as a hook, but not all students necessarily contribute to the response.* *Hunter may have intended universal student participation, but this is seldom the reality in classrooms.*
N—The teacher presents **new information** to students through lecture, video, readings, or demonstrations. Students take notes, generate questions that they clarify with peers or the class as a whole, and use nonlinguistic representations to show the knowledge in a different way. —If the information is *procedural knowledge*, the students are given steps and guided practice. — If the information is *declarative knowledge*, the students gather and organize it and learn or review the steps of a thinking (inquiry) skill.	• Summarizing and note taking • Cooperative learning • Nonlinguistic representations • (Homework and) practice	*In the Hunter model, teachers expect students to listen and take notes, but they are not directed to pause to allow students to ask questions, pair and share, examine images or video, or explain or edit notes based on their interactions with others.* *The Hunter model encourages teachers to check for understanding and monitor and adjust instructional approaches. GANAG does, too, but it also provides opportunities for students to receive some of that feedback from peers and self.*

FIGURE 2.1—(continued)

The GANAG Lesson Plan Format That Includes High-Yield Strategies

Phase Description	High-Yield Strategies	Notes
A—The teacher gives students an opportunity to practice a procedural goal or **apply** the thinking/inquiry skill to a declarative goal. This is the pivotal aspect of the lesson design. When applying declarative knowledge, students can learn to follow thinking skills steps and use them to generate new ideas.	• (Homework and) practice • Identifying similarities and differences • Generating and testing hypotheses • Questions, cues, and advance organizers	*In the Hunter schema, all knowledge appears to be eligible for practice. In GANAG, the goal of the lesson determines the application. If the learning intention for the class is procedural, then the students practice with guidance and independently. If the learning intention for the class is declarative, then the students learn and use a thinking skill.*
G—Before the lesson ends, students re-assess their knowledge and performance on the **goal** as well as their effort to see how well they learned.	• Setting objectives and providing feedback • Reinforcing effort and providing recognition	*"Closure" is a step Hunter added later, after the model was first published, and the reality is that many teachers struggle to stop before the end of the period to summarize the learning. GANAG teaches students that they have a voice – they can self-assess for personal benefit but also to provide feedback to the teacher.*

By shifting the focus of planning lessons from what the teacher does (Mastery Teaching) to what students learn to know and do (Master Learners), and by including steps for deliberately teaching thinking skills, GANAG provides a lesson plan and delivery schema that sets the foundation for inquiry teaching—which is another way to say "i5-ing lesson."

The i5 Lesson

When the i5 approach is applied to the GANAG lesson plan, the result typically looks something like this:

The Beginning of the Lesson

G—The teacher projects the **goal** (declarative or procedural) for the lesson on the electronic whiteboard or directs the class to a website that each student can access on a digital device. Students write in notebooks or type the goal on an electronic goal sheet, self-assess, and share their results with a peer. Students also gauge their habits of mind by assessing how much effort they plan to expend on the learning. To emphasize the "master learners" aspect of GANAG, teaching students goal setting helps them personalize the goal, activating their frontal lobe activity to seek *information* and feedback about how they progress on the goal.

The Middle of the Lesson

A—The students view an *image* or nonlinguistic representation likely projected on the whiteboard or tablet and respond to a planned cue or question about the content. The technique of **accessing prior knowledge** intends for students to think about what they know in anticipation of acquiring new information. Students write their individual responses in a notebook or on a tablet, and then *interact* with partners to clarify their thinking.

N—The students learn **new information** via a lecture from the teacher, a video, a website, or a demonstration. The content may include new declarative knowledge (such as health, science, or humanities topics) or new procedural knowledge (such as how to format a document or how to compose a drawing using negative space). Students use a digital device to search the internet for more *information* or *images* and take notes. Students *interact* by seeking clarification and more *information* from others through wikis, e-mail, or other social media with their digital devices. If the lesson's goal is declarative knowledge, the teacher explicitly teaches or reviews the steps for one of the 12 thinking skills.

The Independent Task

A—Students **apply** procedural knowledge by practicing it in new situations. Technology provides students with access to more and better feedback or *interaction*, more *information* to improve their performance, and *images* to clarify or extend their practice. Students learning declarative knowledge apply their new information using an *inquiry* or thinking skill. A robust task can require students to search for more *information*, make meaning by seeing or creating *images*, and *interact* with others to clarify or seek feedback about their understanding. Through the *inquiry* process, students produce original ideas, or *innovate*.

The End of the Lesson

G—When the lesson ends, students engage in a **goal review**, revisiting the goal and assessing how well they learned and how much effort they expended. They share their progress or *interact* with the teacher through goal sheets.

The Importance of Flexibility

Just as Madeline Hunter admonished teachers to use common sense when implementing her model, we want to add a word about the importance of flexibility and thinking outside of the box when employing GANAG. It is our natural tendency to follow directions, but remember what you already know: Every lesson-planning model is a guideline that can (and should) be adapted to suit the needs of your classroom. Rather than adhere dogmatically to the G-A-N-A-G step progression, consider using common sense to place more emphasis where it is needed or just to vary the routine. For example, the lessons you plan over the course of the week might look like this:

Monday: GANAG
Tuesday: GANaG—more gathering information, minimal application
Wednesday: GANaG
Thursday: AGNaG—for fun, flip the G and A
Friday: GAnAG—less gathering information and more time to apply the thinking skill

Or, on any day, even GAnananaG—teach a little, practice a little, teach a little, apply a little.

Essential Reminders

When considering how you might use the i5 approach to upgrade your lessons and develop the thinking skills, remember the following points about its components:

- *Information:* It's impossible to think about nothing (unless you are George Costanza on *Seinfeld*). The more information that students can access about a topic, the greater their chance of understanding the concept and being positioned to apply their knowledge productively.
- *Images:* Seeing is believing. Being able to view an image or see a video of something in progress gives students more sensory knowledge about the topic; this kicks off the chain of association.
- *Interaction:* Two heads are better than one. Pairing students frequently for clarifications and incorporating shared online sites into instructional activities enriches the information and the feedback they take in.
- *Inquiry:* We have heard the admonition to "think harder" for years, but it's very possible your students have not been taught to approach inquiry as a series of steps. With the help of technology, we can now make thinking an instructional focus.
- *Innovation:* New ideas do not spring miraculously from the ether; they are generated by thinkers based on experiences and information. Students can and should practice innovation every day by gathering information and making productive associations.

Summary

Teachers are expected to encourage students to use technology in ways that are visible in the classroom. When the teacher and students use technology to acquire information, view images, and interact with others, the class becomes more motivating for both parties. But to implement technology effectively and in ways that will deepen student learning, we need to examine how to incorporate technology and the i5 into commonly used models of lesson planning.

The i5 approach helps students use technology as a tool to gather more information and images to extend their understanding, and interact for more timely and personalized feedback. Although both procedural and declarative knowledge can be taught using a thoughtful combination of the i5 and these models, the updated GANAG is especially useful for these purposes, as it provides the option for modeling and practice or cues the teacher to deliberately teach thinking skills so students apply the knowledge in a meaningful way to innovate or generate new ideas.

In the next four chapters, we will explore the inquiry skills, explaining why to teach them, examining the steps in the processes, looking at classroom illustrations, and highlighting the "i5 epiphanies" of teachers who have embraced this approach.

Teaching the Skills of Association

Looking out the window, Jane noticed four students crossing the street one behind the other, one barefoot; it reminded her of *Abbey Road*, the iconic Beatles' album cover.

Did mentioning *Abbey Road* immediately bring to mind the image of four men on a London crosswalk, one of them barefoot? That detail alone may begin to trigger teenage memories for some of you who spent days listening carefully to lyrics and scrutinizing album covers to find clues as to whether the rumor—that "Paul Is Dead"—was true.

Then your mind starts churning, remembering the rumor that Paul McCartney died in a car accident. Had the Fab Four covered this up and replaced McCartney with a look-alike named Billy Shears? It was said that the album cover depicted a funeral procession. Fans saw John dressed in white as a preacher, Ringo in black as a funeral director, and George in denim as the gravedigger. The barefoot Paul was the corpse, because in some cultures, the dead are buried without shoes. From the police van to the blue dress on the back cover, from the cigarette in Paul's right hand to the license plate, the *Abbey Road* cover art presented all kinds of clues that could be interpreted as confirmation that Paul McCartney had died. And although "Paul Is Dead" may have been a hoax or an elaborate marketing scheme, here's a truth that is undeniable: association is real.

Why Teach Association?

The human brain connects what is known to us from our past with what we sense in the present. In his book about the anatomy of the brain, *Beyond the Zonules of Zinn*, David Bainbridge (2008) explains that the cerebral cortex engages high-level linking of lower-level sensory processing—what we see, hear, touch, taste, and smell—to establish context and interpretation. Bainbridge calls this high-level linking, "association" and adds that "there is a great deal of space for all that tantalizing 'association' to go on, in the large cerebral cortex of a human" (p. 274). It is within that "great deal of space" that we hope our students make associations to the topics we teach.

In general terms, the prefrontal cortex conducts the traffic of both physical and mental activity, receiving inputs and determining action. The hippocampus cross-references all new information with existing memories, and those collections of associations are reported back to the conductor to decide whether to act, to move, or to forget.

The fact that association is such a natural and necessary part of surviving in a world of sensory information might answer the question of why teaching using association seems fairly easy to do. Often quoted, Hebb's catchphrase about learning new information speaks directly to this action: "Neurons that fire together, wire together" (Panksepp & Biven, 2012). When stimulated by new information, clusters of neurons are more likely to fire together simultaneously, again helping us make sense (provide context, perceive, and interpret) by remembering a host of other associations instead of just single facts. Association provides increased neural currency, so it makes sense to teach it explicitly when students are learning new declarative information.

How do we use information about the Beatles, brain research, and brainstorming by association as a practical tactic for teaching lessons that target thinking? In this chapter, we'll look at strategies to help students develop three inquiry skills that target association—**comparing, classifying**, and **creating analogies**—and at classroom examples of how the i5 approach galvanizes innovation.

Comparing

Comparing is the "simple connection" part of association. Finding similarities and differences among the topics or products around us is a practical way to deal with the flood of incoming information or sensory data. In *Classroom Instruction That Works* (Marzano et al., 2001), Jane and her colleagues identified the strategy of finding similarities and differences between and among items as having a high probability of increasing student learning ($d = 1.61$). Students have a much greater chance of retaining information and being able to use it to generate new ideas when they find associations or similarities and differences among items.

Ask yourself: What kinds of **comparing tasks** do you assign, and for what purposes? Then, with these tasks in mind, ask yourself the **i5 questions**:

1. How else could the students and I search for *information?*
2. How else could we use visual *images* and nonlinguistic representations to add meaning?
3. How could I encourage students to *interact* with others, live or through social media, to obtain and provide feedback?
4. How could I teach the *inquiry* skill—comparing—to deepen knowledge?
5. How could I plan for the students to use the application to generate *innovative* insights and products related to the lesson goals?

The Procedure

The first instinct when teaching comparison might be to give directions for filling in a Venn diagram, or sketch out a process that looks like this:

1. Identify two items.
2. Indicate what about them is similar.
3. Indicate what about them is different.
4. Draw a conclusion and produce a product.

Reasonable, right? Except that following those steps leads students to describe obvious parallels and not venture very deeply into the content. Notably, what's missing is the pivotal step that transforms comparing into a higher-order inquiry process. Figure 3.1 shows a better alternative—the steps involved in making a higher-order comparison. Specifically look at Step 2. Note that when you're teaching this skill— or any other—it can help to translate the steps into simpler or more

---

FIGURE 3.1
How to Compare

The objective: Describe how items are the same or different.

Steps in the Process	Simplified Language
1. Identify the items to compare. (Comparing three or more items makes the comparison more ambiguous and, therefore, more complex.)	1. Name the items to compare.
2. Identify features by which to associate the items.	2. Tell some features about the items.
3. State how the items are similar or different based on the features.	3. Say how the items are the same or different based on the features.
4. Summarize findings to generate new ideas or insights.	4. Tell what you know now (share a new idea) or could do with the information (create a new product).

student-friendly language, especially in the elementary grades and with English language learners. We've provided a simplified-language version of this skill in the figure (see column 2) and will do so for all the thinking skills addressed in the chapters ahead.

The pivotal step in the comparison process that marks the transition from simple recall to higher-order thinking is Step 2, identifying features or characteristics that will serve as the basis for comparison. Teachers can teach students how to identify unusual characteristics to deliver a more complex comparison. For example, say we're setting out to compare world leaders. At first, one might consider intellect, previous accomplishments, or grit. But, to press on, one might consider factors such as

- Responses to controversial international events
- Noteworthy or unique initiatives set into motion
- Examples of humility or humanitarianism

Naming these features provides motivation to search for the *information* and view *images* or videos of evidence. Considering each leader by each feature drives us to *interact* with others to clarify the accuracy of the information to further define the topic, check perceptions using new sources, and seek other interpretations. This *inquiry* process generates new insights or *innovative ideas*—from which one can form well-supported opinions about what makes the best kind of world leader. To increase the complexity of students' comparison inquiry, remember the "rule of three." In a comparison of two items, one will naturally appear "better." Adding a third item adds ambiguity that requires the thinker to seek out more information, make more connections, and reach more nuanced conclusions.

Notice that the last step in comparison combines generating a summary of findings and generating original thoughts. Remember Goldberg's mermaid example from a previous chapter. You do not need your frontal lobes to recall a fish or a girl from memory, but when you use your frontal lobes to link those memories, you can generate a mermaid. In his example, the mermaid is likely something you have not experienced before; it is the new idea. All thinking tasks, then, could properly end with new ideas since that is what our brains can naturally do when we make associations in everyday life. As a practical illustration, the task of comparing world leaders might conclude with students creating a job description for the next head of state instead of just summarizing the information they've collected about the leaders.

Once students have learned and practiced the skill of comparison, it can be a useful tool for assessment. This is a case where a two-item comparison can be a better choice than a three-item comparison for the sake of delimiting the task to the time frame of a test. For example, a test might ask students to "compare two of the world leaders from among the many we have studied."

In the Classroom: Lesson Examples

Author Study

Susan Hensley, the contributing author of this book, worked with 3rd grade teachers to introduce the work of author Jan Brett to students. Susan commented that often class "discussions" consisted mostly of teachers telling students about setting, central messages, and characters' responses to events or challenges and then accepting restatements of the points she or he had provided.

To introduce the i5 approach, Susan started to search online for an image of Jan Brett and wound up spending nearly an hour on the author's website, which is rich with blog posts, videos, steps to drawing a hedgehog, and descriptions of more than 30 books. Susan had an i5 epiphany. Asking students to access the website of the author would be a way to address the standards *conduct a short research project to build knowledge about a topic, recall information from experiences, or gather information from print and digital sources* and *take brief notes on sources and sort evidence into provided categories.*

With the i5 in mind, Susan suggested that teachers read one of Jan Brett's stories aloud to their students but then show them how to access information from the author's website—including the *images* there and the opportunities to *interact* with the author and her readers. The website also presents *information* about Brett's travels and how traveling inspires her work. As a class, students could generate questions they had about the author based on what they had learned from the website.

One thing students would discover is that Brett chooses a place to visit and study before she writes a children's story about that location. They planned to have the students read three more books and compare them on the bases of the setting, the characters, and the author's language styles. They also planned to have the students access the website for digital information about the author and her specific writing techniques. By comparing various books (*inquiry*), the teachers could guide the students to predict what setting the author might write about next and what types of characters would occupy the new setting.

The final task in the author study was a class collaboration calling for students to draft a letter to Jan Brett suggesting a new idea: that she write about their town and offer a locally-inspired theme and colloquial characters (*innovation*).

The i5 Reflection: The images and information Susan found while exploring Jan Brett's website were so compelling that she instantly understood the power of the i5 to encourage teachers to plan for students to benefit from the same experience. During the first lesson session, she and the teachers realized that although many of her students used digital devices for entertainment, few seemed to be aware that they could use the internet to look up an author or interact with information on a more academic level.

"The i5 reminds me to put the information, images, and interaction in the hands and minds of the students if I want them to use thinking skills," said one of the teachers. "It shifts young students from using technology for fun to using technology to learn."

Roller Coasters and Solar Panels

Ian Mulligan, a high school physics teacher, loved retelling the story (or maybe the urban legend) about the physics students at Harvard who could pass tests about formulas but were unable to fix the window blinds that hung askew. "Those could have been my students," he told us, "at least, they could have been before I started teaching thinking rather than just expecting it from my students."

In the past, Mr. Mulligan's lectures on the difference between potential and kinetic energy consisted mostly of how to apply formulas. He would give the quintessential example of the roller coaster going up and down to show the different types of energy. Students seemed to enjoy the animation of the roller coaster video and did well on the calculations. However, closer examination revealed that they were unable to imagine other examples of who would use the formulas to make or improve products or ideas. He decided that the i5 approach would target the applied understanding or students' ability to see potential and kinetic energy in real-world examples.

To begin, Mr. Mulligan showed a drawing from the 1500s, credited to da Vinci, of a trebuchet launching stones, fire, and dead animals over a castle wall. His point was that potential and kinetic energy was not new—and had been applied in odd ways over centuries. As Mr. Mulligan had done in the past, he taught the formulas and lectured about energy (*information*). This time, he asked students to search for potential and kinetic energy online, but to do it via an image search. They found examples as different as satellites in orbit, shooting arrows, and beating hearts (*images*). Mr. Mulligan set up a class chat (*interaction*) with a homework assignment where students could post *information* and ask questions or hypothesize about real-world situations in preparation for in-class discussion.

Next up was the lesson's inquiry task, set up to engage students in comparing the examples they'd gathered. After teaching the steps of comparison, Mr. Mulligan asked students to compare different products that might then be improved when applying the knowledge of potential and kinetic energy. Mr. Mulligan showed students how to search online for "thinking maps," and found many different examples of organizers suitable for various grade levels and subject areas. He found it useful to support students' working through the steps of thinking by providing a graphic organizer to compile the information about a topic.

Mr. Mulligan found that the more *images* and videos of soccer kicks, bridge designs, volcanic eruptions, and ice skating students saw to explain movement, the more technical vocabulary they sought to use in their searches and in their discussions of findings with peers (*interaction*). One student pair created a matrix (*inquiry: comparing*) of different solar panel systems. They compared the systems based on materials, layouts, positioning, and size, and used what they had learned about energy to make suggestions for improvement to the products. In the end, all the students personalized their tasks by showing the products and sharing ways that the companies should change their designs (*innovation*).

The i5 Reflection: Mr. Mulligan's "aha" in teaching physics came when he realized that one or two examples are not enough for students to understand abstract concepts well enough to generate their own ideas about them. By searching and reading online, his students engaged with varied examples; the more they viewed, the more questions they asked, and the better they began to understand the application of potential and kinetic energy. The pivot step of identifying features expanded the students' range of products to compare. Teaching comparison led them to more deeply understand how things work and how those things might be improved.

Mr. Mulligan noted that technology can provide more feedback than a single teacher can generate alone. Students can get feedback by working in pairs or groups, and by searching, they can provide self-feedback. When provided with a challenging task, students search for images and information, some may be off-base, but they learn through those missteps. Because students are online, at any moment, all of them can view the same example with a link or on a shared document. The immediacy and flexibility of using technology provides motivation that keeps even the most social adolescent focused on the goal of the lesson.

Classifying

Scientists classify living things to help explain relationships among plants and animals and make predictions; department stores classify and reclassify products to help shoppers locate products and encourage them to buy more; nutritionists classify foods to help us make healthy choices. We might classify spices in the kitchen cabinet, shoes in the closet, or tools in the shed. Often classifying, like other inquiry processes, leads to simple, yet useful discoveries. Grouping items by like characteristics and then regrouping them is a skill that helps us understand the world in which we live.

The associations we make when classifying, coupled with existing memory and emotion, allow us to decide whether to keep the information to store as memory, filter it, or even use it as a launching point for inquiry. Most important—and this is a great part about being human—the movement of this declarative knowledge, the association and re-association with prior knowledge, prompts us to transform the inputs we receive into a new understanding or ideas: something that is ours, informed by our memories and experiences. The periodic table, for example, is not a static old classifying system, but a dynamic classification that motivates scientists to search and create more elements (Kean, 2010). If that is the case, then areas other than science could provide students with similar motivation to generate new ideas. Why not classify tools in a design class, software programs, masterpieces, diseases, or words to see if the associations help students understand the topic more deeply, retain the information better, and possibly generate insights that motivate them to learn more or create a new product?

Ask yourself: What kinds of **classifying tasks** do you assign, and for what purposes? Then, with these tasks in mind, ask yourself the **i5 questions**:

1. How else could the students and I search for *information?*
2. How else could we use visual *images* and nonlinguistic representations to add meaning?
3. How could I encourage students to *interact* with others, live or through social media, to obtain and provide feedback?
4. How could I teach the *inquiry* skill—classifying—to deepen knowledge?
5. How could I plan for the students to use the application to generate *innovative* insights and products related to the lesson goals?

The Procedure

Some information we teach is already classified in a standardized way (e.g., the scientific classification in biology or titles in a genre) and we also teach classifying as a skill to understand why it is so important to know that element and animal classifications are standard. But we can teach students to classify as a thinking skill, sort and regroup items on their own, fine-tune details, clear up misconceptions, and draw insights about the topic. Whereas in a comparison, the association process is driven by making a one-to-one correspondence between (and among) items on single features, classifying is best applied when large numbers of items are grouped according to combined features. Figure 3.2 shows the steps of classifying to teach to students and incorporate into lessons.

Classifying is a skill students can use whenever there are multiple factors to consider.

FIGURE 3.2
How to Classify

The objective: Group items together based on shared traits.

Steps in the Process	Simplified Language
1. Identify multiple items to sort.	1. Name items to classify.
2. Sort the items based on a single or multiple attributes.	2. Sort the items and say why they are in a group.
3. Reorganize or regroup items.	3. Say how items could go into different groups.
4. Summarize findings to generate new ideas or products.	4. Tell what you know now (share a new idea) or could do with the information (create a new product).

The pivot step in applying classifying as an inquiry skill is Step 3, regrouping. For example, in a speech class, students might view a set of speeches and classify them according to various criteria; regrouping these speeches, they may realize that size of audience impacts the delivery. Students in a primary-grade math class assigned to group triangles might regroup them to see patterns that help them understand how they could use different triangles to measure more efficiently. In a building trade class, students could classify home repairs, and then, when the repairs are regrouped, generate insights on how to prepare an alternate budget based on costs, not time.

In the Classroom: Lesson Examples

America in Conflict

Susan worked with a team of 5th grade teachers to plan an interdisciplinary unit about conflict. *Bull Run,* a book by Paul Fleischman (1993), provides 16 monologues that give life to different perspectives about race, gender, the economy, and social tensions during the U.S. Civil War. Susan suggested that the teachers apply the i5 by focusing on the standard that asks students to "Describe how a narrator's or speaker's point of view influences how events are described." She also pointed out that because *Bull Run* has so many characters, its study would be a great opportunity to use and build classifying skills.

The teachers randomly assigned characters to students. Although everyone would take notes as they listened to online audio of the monologues, they would pay special attention to details about their assigned characters (*information*). The task required students to create a dossier for their character by gathering images and accurate related historical information online; then they formatted the information into an electronic trading card (*information, images*). Students shared the cards online so all students could view each other's character cards (*interaction*).

After teaching the steps to classifying, the teachers helped students brainstorm possible ways to group the characters. Some characters believed that joining the army to fight on front lines was important while others did not share their points of view. Students worked in teams to classify characters based on categories such as gender, geography, action taken, or an event that happened to them (*inquiry: classifying*). The classifying exercise provided time for teachers to listen in to conversations, give feedback, and offer suggestions about creatively reclassifying the characters as a way to deeply understand the conflict they studied.

After the activity, the students were asked to summarize their understanding of *Bull Run* and also comment about today's world (*innovation*). Would different people share points of view if they were different genders or race? What might make some people disagree, even if they were in similar occupations? The students were then able to transfer what they knew to more current situations.

The i5 Reflection: Planning to teach a thinking skill can change a good lesson with good materials into a great lesson where students tease out the nuances of the content. Students leave an activity like this one with a heightened awareness that those on different sides of a conflict can have very similar ideas. With access to the audio monologues and images, students could visualize the speakers and their plights; they could see the geography, the housing, and even the distance that some spoke of traveling. Although the *information* from the readings online was engaging for the student groups (*interaction*), and the *images* were revealing, the *inquiry* task of classifying and reclassifying added an element of tension that increased the students' interest in the topic of the Civil War and its impact on everyday people.

Sorting Cells

Classifying tasks are a staple of Veronica Armstrong's lessons. "Picture yourself back in biology class learning about cells," she told us. "Your teacher probably handed you that two-dimensional, black-and-white diagram of a rectangular plant cell and a round animal cell and asked you to label the parts. I want my students to understand these concepts more deeply by shifting students' role from memorizing material to being active thinkers."

Using the i5 approach, Ms. Armstrong showed students 10 electron micrographs of each cell type (*images*) from online sources. She taught students to use the Cell Image Library (cellimagelibrary.org) and the Cell-Centered Database (www.ccdb.ucsd.edu) to gather more examples (*information*), which they classified based on their knowledge of the characteristics of cells as well as organelles (*inquiry: classifying*). The benefit to using the online resources was the number of possibilities it opened; its vast stores of images could lead to all kinds of questions and understandings. Because students worked on a shared drive, Ms. Armstrong could give them real-time feedback, and students could seek feedback from peers as well (*interaction*).

"My goal is to challenge students to go beyond just labeling and explaining the parts of cells to understanding the functions of the parts, so that they can generate new ideas or deduce functions that may not yet be confirmed (*innovation*)," Ms. Armstrong explained. "Changing my old task to a classifying task worked since the online resource offers almost unlimited material. This *inquiry* gave students many more opportunities to genuinely ask questions about types of cells and functions rather than asking me for directions about how to fill in the old paper organizer."

The i5 Reflection: Before digital technology was commonplace in the classroom, it was customary for students to view a limited number of slides while sharing a limited number of microscopes; now students can view dozens of common and unusual images online. Online databases provide more information than students can find in classroom sets of print materials and provide links to other sites where students can find answers to questions that arise as they engage in thinking tasks. This lesson illustrates how using technology to access resources can transform science tasks, and how the use of common performance space (a shared drive) can facilitate timely feedback from both teacher and peers.

Creating Analogies

Analogies are ways that we make the unfamiliar familiar and that make new information easier to understand. Recalling a past situation provides concrete images, and we are able to connect new information to existing understandings. With this experience or knowledge now enlisted, we can think more clearly about a new situation. It's remarkable how adept we are at recognizing highly diverse domains that have only the slightest thread of a common connection: the leader is a rhino, dinner smells like heaven, the melody is like the tides, and so on.

In *Shortcut: How Analogies Reveal Connections, Spark Innovation, and Sell Our Greatest Ideas* (2015), John Pollack writes about great figures in business who famously used analogies to create empires—for example, Steve Jobs of Apple. In the 1980s, Jobs gave a speech about what Apple was going to do to sell computers. He talked about a study that he had read in *Scientific American* focused on comparing the speeds of animals. Interestingly, he said, while others collected data about the animals, one scientist thought to test a human on a bicycle; the human on the bike vaulted into the top spot of the standings, achieving the highest speed while expending the least amount of energy. Humans, Jobs noted, are toolmakers; they could augment an inherent ability with a tool. The tool he was focused on, he said, would be the computer—the bicycle for the mind.

Pollack states that analogies may often go unnoticed, but they are nonetheless arguments, albeit "arguments that, like icebergs, conceal most of their mass and power beneath the surface. In many arguments, whoever has the best analogy wins" (pp. xiv–xv). Teachers can teach students to go below the surface by teaching them the steps for and practicing mining information by creating their own analogies.

Ask yourself: What kinds of **analogy-creation tasks** do you assign, and for what purposes? Then, with these tasks in mind, ask yourself the **i5 questions**:

1. How else could the students and I search for *information?*
2. How else could we use visual *images* and nonlinguistic representations to add meaning?
3. How could I encourage students to *interact* with others, live or through social media, to obtain and provide feedback?
4. How could I teach the *inquiry* skill—creating analogies—to deepen knowledge?
5. How could I plan for the students to use the application to generate *innovative* insights and products related to the lesson goals?

The Procedure

Creating an analogy involves noting and using the relationship between two similar situations to produce a deeper understanding. Analogies can be a word, a metaphor or a simile, or an entire story line.

Journalists use them frequently and often deftly. You might read a news story where, either explicitly or implicitly, the journalist describes someone as an ogre or a situation as a Cinderella story. These remind you of fairy tales that provide you with insight into a predictable ending. The analogy guides you to speculate well before the writer states what actually happened.

Teachers have many opportunities to teach students to strengthen this inquiry skill in any grade level or subject; it is likely all students will have some common memories, and that is a solid start. Figure 3.3 shows the steps of creating analogies.

FIGURE 3.3
How to Create Analogies

The objective: Identify a relationship or pattern between a known and an unknown situation.

Steps in the Process	Simplified Language
1. Identify an event or topic that is difficult to understand.	1. Tell about a topic that is hard to understand.
2. Identify a familiar situation describing the steps or the parts in general terms.	2. Explain a familiar story or experience in your own words.
3. Explain the new event or topic using the familiar situation to guide the narrative.	3. Tell how each part of what you know works, so you can explain the new topic.
4. Summarize understandings and generate insights about the new event or topic.	4. Tell what you know now (share a new idea) or could do with the information (create a new product).

Because analogies often involve engaging an audience, the pivot step that prompts thinking is finding the right familiar situation to reveal the iceberg below. As a caution, we remember a teacher telling us that when teaching 7th graders, she referred to the characters in the junior literature book as Macbeth-like, hoping to excite the students and generate discussion. Instead, the students fell silent. Since they were not familiar with *Macbeth* (as they might have been with a *Romeo and*

Juliet reference), they could not follow through with the analogy. "Double, double toil and trouble"—literally!

If you identify the right familiar story or experience, then you can methodically connect each part of a familiar concept to a new one. That marks the moment when you use what you know to actively process the new situation; you begin to think. When we teach to students to make analogies when they encounter new information, we equip them to intentionally connect it to prior knowledge to generate new and deeper understandings. What makes analogies creative is that you can also add twists or turns to the relationships, generating surprises in the result. For example, when reporting about a politician in the news using "The Emperor's New Clothes" as the familiar sequence of events, the journalist may surprise the reader by divulging that at the end of the day, that politician was really the little boy, and not the emperor.

When we work with teachers to plan lessons to teach thinking skills, we use an analogy. We describe the frontal lobes as the brain's Swiss Army knife. The knife has blades, a screwdriver, a can opener, and other versatile tools stowed in the handle with a pivot mechanism; the frontal lobes involve the use of thinking skills. Different tools work for different situations. When you need to cut a piece of rope, you use a blade or the scissors. For planning instruction, you may choose to address the situation by solving it as a problem, or you may choose to analyze perspectives. The Swiss Army analogy allows us to view thinking skills as specific tools, some of which work better than others given the subject area. It should also encourage teachers to avoid "binging" on skills and try different thinking skills in lessons.

In the Classroom: Lesson Examples

The Ecosystem and the Government

Carla Hemmers teaches 3rd graders. In the beginning of the school year, her students learned about habitats and different ecosystems; they learned about interdependence. To deepen understanding, they gathered online *information* and *images* of forests, tundra, deserts, and so on and used Glogster (http://edu.glogster.com) to create interactive multimedia posters that show how interdependence works in ecosystems.

In the second term, Ms. Hemmers's students studied the functions of the local government in social studies class. Because of the interdependence of people in government, she saw this lesson as an opportunity to teach analogy (*inquiry*). Following the steps in the process, the class revisited the familiar concept of ecosystems. Then they identified the new situation as people and government and systematically used information from the familiar to learn how parts of the town government work together. Ms. Hemmers was surprised when the students asked questions extending the analogy to state and national government systems. As the students worked through the analogy, they found they needed to go online to find *information* and *images* that would provide an explanation. The students used Ed.VoiceThread, a collaborative presentation app (http://voicethread.com/products/k12/) to showcase their statements that began with this prompt: "_____ is to a government like _____ is to an ecosystem" (*innovation*). Other students could ask questions or clarify their analogies (*interaction*). In summarizing their work, students could see how schools and households might also be said to have the same traits as both the ecosystem and government, because they also were composed of people who depended on one another.

The i5 Reflection: Ms. Hemmers was amazed at how 3rd graders could use information from an earlier science lesson to transfer to the topic of governments. She also said that she expected her students to produce similar examples, but the students seemed motivated to create something unique, spurred on by having access to one another's work. The online digital conversation and interactions with other students enriched their discussions, but it also allowed Ms. Hemmers time to formatively assess the students as they worked on their analogies, clarifying the content and correcting any misunderstandings.

The Brain Is Not Like a Computer

When a PLT (professional learning team) in Psychology and Humanities at a secondary school asked us to help them apply the i5 to teaching about the human cognitive system, or how the brain works, it led to a slight adjustment in their lessons. Here's a look at what we planned.

First, teachers in their own classes asked students to search online, in pairs, for images of computers and generate a list showing five parts and functions of a computers (*images, information, interaction*). Then, they showed a 30-second video of a busy hotel lobby, in which the camera panned up to show a glass elevator with people heading up to their rooms. The next slide featured a quotation from Massachusetts Institute of Technology memory expert Suzanne Corkin: "Our brains are like hotels with eclectic arrays of guests—homes to different kinds of memory, each of which occupies its own suite of rooms" (2013, p. 51). A few minutes later, they presented a slide showing a photo of an orchestra and quoted neuroscientist Elkhonon Goldberg (2009) describing the brain's prefrontal cortex as the conductor: Humans learn by making connections between and among pieces of information. The prefrontal cortex is the brain boss, or the conductor of the orchestra of learning.

The teachers posed a question to the class: *Which best depicts the structure and function of the human brain—a computer, a hotel, or an orchestra?* The ultimate task, they explained, would be for students to build their own analogy (*innovation*) to describe the workings of the brain as they studied the structure and function of the human cognitive system. They could use *information* and *images* they found online to expand their analogies, ranging from ant colonies to subway systems. This allowed them to include details beyond what was presented to them in class, and they created slide decks that they shared on the class website. Students also provided feedback on each other's assignments online by asking questions related to the cognitive parts or functions as shown in the analogies (*interaction*).

The i5 Reflection: In the past, these teachers would have provided one analogy to the students. The i5 approach's advocacy of including inquiry skill instruction to generate new iterations or uses of knowledge gave them a framework to teach students to be creative, but also accurate, when explaining brain functions. Updating their lesson plans to enlist technology made this possible, as it was the technology that gave students access to the additional imagery and information that fueled their creativity, and their analogies.

Summary

The skills of association empower students to transform declarative knowledge presented to them into deeper and more personal understanding. To be more specific, two types of learning happen when students associate. First, they connect new ideas they're encountering in the lesson to established knowledge and prior experiences, increasing the likelihood they'll retain new information. Second, students become more *efficient* at making these connections, setting themselves up to be increasingly adept thinkers who will likely generate productive ideas and discoveries. Association is fundamental to how we function in our daily lives, so to address it in our study of inquiry skills is a logical starting point.

Teaching the Skills of Synthesis

Ten years ago, Dr. Ginger Campbell began hosting *The Brain Science Podcast* (www.brainsciencepodcast.com), which she describes as a podcast for "anyone who has a brain." An emergency room physician for more than 20 years, Campbell dates her interest in neuroscience to when developments in imaging technology began to reveal new insights into the mind and brain and dispel several conclusions long held within the field.

In her monthly podcast, Dr. Campbell reviews books and interviews authors in the field of neuroscience about their latest works, addressing such topics such as brain plasticity, the story and science of the reading brain, the world of sleep, and why humans feel disgust. Not surprisingly, after years of reading and chatting with writers about these topics, Campbell produced her own book, *Are You Sure? The Unconscious Origins of Certainty* (2012). As she says on her podcast, she never *planned* to write the book, but she felt compelled to share insights sparked by all the information she had been absorbing. Over many years, Dr. Campbell began to extract themes from all that she had been reading and learning about, and finally she synthesized them into her own, original take on the topic.

As humans, we can process enormous amounts of information. When we do, we can use synthesis to find threads or themes and convert them into unique insights.

Why Teach Synthesis?

In the often-quoted *Taxonomy of Educational Objectives*, edited by Benjamin Bloom (1956), the authors identify synthesis as an element near the top of the hierarchy of thinking. They define synthesis as "the putting together of elements and parts so as to form a whole. This involves the process of working with pieces, parts, elements, etc., and arranging and combining them in such a way as to constitute a pattern or structure not clearly there before" (p. 206). This definition underscores that synthesis not only provides a way to make productive use of the vast amount of information available via the internet, it is also a driving force behind *innovation*. As educators, we work to develop students' capacity to innovate because of the advantage it affords them in a rapidly changing world.

There are two inquiry skills we can teach students to support their ability to synthesize: **investigating** and **constructing an argument**. As we will see, the critical active thinking step in an investigation is not the searching (gathering and organizing information) but the finding: zooming in on a confusion, an ambiguity, or an unusual aspect about the information that leads an individual to generate a new explanation. The point of asking students to take in lots of information is not so that they will be able to reproduce it verbatim later, but so that they can use that information to make their own interpretation. They do this by identifying common themes and then generating their own explanations or versions of those themes. Constructing an argument is a similar process of transformative creation. Many people would categorize argument as "analysis or breaking something into smaller parts," but it makes more sense to us as a skill that requires synthesis. Students gather and organize evidence from diverse sources of information, including having to consider counterclaims or concessions; they need a process to combine these elements into a cohesive new whole by proposing a claim and then offering the whole as a set of information.

Using the i5 approach—asking students to gather information and images online, interact with the material, and engage in interactive discussion of what they do and do not understand about it—creates an environment conducive to developing synthesis skills.

Investigating

Sir Arthur Conan Doyle, an unemployed medical surgeon when he took up writing, created Sherlock Holmes, the quintessential master of investigation. Doyle couched Holmes's investigation technique in suspenseful narratives, providing readers the experience of gathering evidence and synthesizing understanding as he revealed only bits of information at a time. Holmes always seemed to know "who done it" all along, but the reader had to work to figure this out, sorting out the confusing factors until the patterns, and the culprit, came into focus.

The television news magazine *60 Minutes* is a modern-day exemplar of the value of investigation. Unlike the daily news and "just the facts" approach, investigative journalists crave the contradiction in a story, the confusion about the evidence, and the unique or unusual circumstances that make the facts of the case ambiguous. Wherever there is ambiguity, thinking thrives. These journalists gather assorted information, organize it, and present their verified findings as a creative solution to variations of "What is really going on here?" An investigation involves parsing the details to see what might reveal itself as a pattern.

Not all investigations are macabre or even mysterious. Coming up with a better definition of a conceptual idea is an investigation (e.g., "What is personalization?" "What does it mean to be media literate?"). So is answering a speculative question ("What would human life look like on Mars?"). So is explaining a literary technique ("What roles do archetypes play in the novels of William Faulkner?") or a historical event ("What were the lasting effects of the Colorado Gold Rush of 1858?"). Any time you want students to transform something "known by others" into something *they know themselves* is an opportunity for investigation. These are the kinds of active and creative tasks that teachers plan for students to engage in when applying the skill of investigation.

Ask yourself: What kinds of **investigation tasks** do you assign, and for what purposes? Then, with these tasks in mind, ask yourself the **i5 questions**:

1. How else could the students and I search for *information?*
2. How else could we use visual *images* and nonlinguistic representations to add meaning?
3. How could I encourage students to *interact* with others, live or through social media, to obtain and provide feedback?
4. How could I teach the *inquiry* skill—investigating—to deepen knowledge?
5. How could I plan for the students to use the application to generate *innovative* insights and products related to the lesson goals?

The Procedure

The skills we use to synthesize or extract themes are useful for interpreting large amounts of information—and clearly, this is a huge help in the areas of humanities or sciences. Art and music teachers can and should teach students to synthesize information about the development of techniques over decades and centuries; math teachers can show students how 17th century mathematicians Wilhelm Liebniz and Isaac Newton independently synthesized what they each knew to create calculus, a method to measure the quantity of curving using infinite series of terms. Figure 4.1 shows the steps of investigating.

FIGURE 4.1
How to Investigate

The objective: Explain the theme of a topic, including anything that is ambiguous or contradictory.

Steps in the Process	Simplified Language
1. Identify a topic to study or research.	1. Describe something or something that happened.
2. State the ambiguity or contradiction about the topic and gather information.	2. Say the main idea about the topic, or what is unique or unusual about it.
3. Clarify the ambiguous or contradictory issues to extract the theme and gather more information, if necessary.	3. Read and gather information to explain the confusion.
4. Summarize understandings and generate insights about the topic.	4. Tell what you know now (share a new idea) or could do with the information (create a new product).

Recall that in each of the association thinking skills discussed in Chapter 3, one step stands out as the pivot point that changes the student's role from passive recipient to active thinker. Investigation is driven by exploring the murkiness of a situation or information. The pivot in this skill process comes in Step 2, when students shift from the relatively simple task of gathering information on a topic to stating an ambiguity or contradiction within that topic. This is when they activate the thinking process and begin to generate questions. In this way, the inquiry skill of investigation is like "imaging"—approaching every sight as a blur that slowly comes into focus as we put the pieces together.

Research projects are all about investigating—or at least they are intended to be. Investigations require research skills, but too often, we define researching as the procedural skill of gathering, citing, and organizing knowledge. Explicitly teaching the synthesis skill of investigation may be the antidote to frustrating student practices like cutting and pasting others' material to use in essays and projects rather than drawing original conclusions, generating individual ideas, and transforming found information into a new understanding. When the research intention involves a process to define or clarify the opacity of a topic, then the motivation for the work becomes so much greater.

In the Classroom: Lesson Examples
The Nation's Birthday

Alina Mejia, preschool teacher at the Mazapan School, an international school in La Ceiba, Honduras, wanted her preschoolers to know the importance of Independence Day. Before being introduced into the i5, Sra. Mejia wrote the standards about national celebrations and developing civic identity, as "I can describe the independence of Honduras." Students would participate in the traditional "Acto Civico," or school program, with a presentation of a dance, "bombas" (famous sayings) and traditional foods. Her students were invariably the cutest act on the program, but she sensed they were missing the deeper significance of a celebration—that it marked a nation's independence. She realized that she kept the students busy "doing activities" but not necessarily learning about, discussing, or asking questions about the concept. Motivated by the i5 approach, she was convinced her students might explore this idea through inquiry.

Others disagreed. When Sra. Mejia brought up the idea of teaching thinking skills to her preschoolers, she was told there was no need—that inquiry skills weren't needed until later school years. This, to her, was a challenge. Were they saying that preschoolers did not think, ask questions, or create new ways of interpreting information? Sra. Mejia was going to conduct her own investigation to find out.

The students enrolled in her school hailed from many countries, so she decided to bring together the celebration of Honduran independence with the independence celebrations of those other countries. Sra. Mejia revised the lesson goal to "I know why Honduras, the United States, and other countries celebrate independence days." She announced to her students that they would be investigating (*inquiry*) the idea of independence (Step 1 of the thinking skill).

Teaching preschool involves a lot of prompting, so she started by accessing prior knowledge with pictures of birthday celebrations (*images*). With students sprawled on the rug in front of the electronic whiteboard, she showed images about birthdays; students saw people gathered around one person and a cake, birthday hats, and games like hitting the piñata. She kept up the prompts ("What is the celebration here?" "Why do we celebrate a birthday?"), and her students kept calling out answers.

Then she showed a new set of images—people gathered together, people wearing mariachi hats, and crowds watching fireworks—some of which she had to explain (*information*). She showed people wearing red, white, and blue, gathered around a barbeque pit. "Turn and talk," she prompted (*interaction*). "Is this also a birthday celebration?" "Does it look like the celebration is about one person... or about something bigger?" Sra. Mejia deliberately created a pivot point there by asking it in such a way to make it sound like *something unique or unusual was going on here.* When she showed the military uniforms and typical dresses for Honduras, the students recognized they were seeing a picture of their independence celebration. "Do countries have birthdays?" Sra. Mejia asked. "Yes!" the preschoolers responded. Even though the thinking process seems a bit forced at the preschool level, Sra. Mejia explained that it was really the first time she had thought to have students learn *about* independence and not simply learn to sing songs and perform.

Together, they made a book online with some words and pictures about countries and their birthdays: their independence days (*innovation*).

The i5 Reflection: Sra. Mejia was so proud of her students, because this year they really grasped the idea of a nation having a celebration similar to a birthday. She said that the i5 gave her the motivation to insist on using a thinking skill. Yes, she had to prompt every step of the way, but searching for information and images online made it so much more productive. "Everyone gives us credit in preschool for having such creative students," she said, "but from now on, they are going to see that we also teach students the critical thinking skills like investigation."

The Mural

It was three weeks before the end of the school year when Frank Korb's Advanced Placement Studio Art class students asked if they could work on a group project that would address all the elements and principles of art they had studied. They wanted a collective way to showcase their individual skills and proposed creating a mural for the social studies computer lab. They would choose the mural materials, size, imagery, and message.

Mr. Korb hesitated, having assigned "group" projects in the past where some students toiled and others talked. He had his students research group project protocols, and they came across *charrettes*— intensive planning sessions that some architectural teams use when they work on a vision together (*information, interaction*).

The students learned about the technique via video and websites, clarifying the steps of working as a charrette. Then students created a timeline for the project that they decided would derive from Michelangelo's *Creation of Adam* (*images*). Despite the preparation, on Day 1, they hit the wall (or the ceiling in this case), with students unsure of how to get started. "I struggled to not be involved," Mr. Korb said, "but I realized that I would have to give them the thinking skills steps to springboard new insights."

To help his students get unstuck and get started, he posted and taught the steps of investigation (*inquiry*). When Mr. Korb got to Step 2, the nature of students' struggle started to become clearer. In hindsight, he said, he was amazed that the group spent so much time talking timelines without ever really considering the experience they would be creating for the viewer. What was the ambiguity in this topic that they wanted to explore? How could they shift their goal from working together to make a mural about the Renaissance to working together to produce a creative project that would be interesting for them, and interesting for viewers? They reset their goal: To create a mural for the computer classroom that would blend Renaissance themes and techniques of the 1500s with 21st century technology (*innovation*).

The process of identifying the themes and contradiction of placing Michelangelo in a computer lab was determined in the charrette. Tasks were assigned to small groups by leaders who continued to direct (*interaction*) while also being fully immersed in the workings of the artwork. The meetings were guided by the investigation protocol: gather materials (*information, images*), state the emerging vision (*interaction*), add more materials, restate the vision, add more, and finalize the vision. In the end, the mural inspired by Michelangelo's *Creation of Adam* installed in the social studies computer lab (*innovation*) was a masterpiece.

The i5 Reflection: Mr. Korb wrote to us saying that his students completed their mural by using the ambiguity of an investigation to "apply ideas of the *Creation of Adam* and tying them in to humans' creation of technology (an apt fit for the computer lab)." Mr. Korb's epiphany can be attributed to Aristotle: *The whole is greater than the sum of its parts.* The whole of the i5 approach (information + images + interaction + inquiry) leads to the innovation.

Constructing an Argument

Mention "teaching thinking," and many teachers will look at you quizzically before nodding that yes, they do teach thinking. When the topic came up, Jill North, an elementary science teacher in Missouri, asked for clarification. "You mean Bloom's taxonomy?" she asked. "Are you asking if I am teaching students to go higher on Bloom's taxonomy?"

Jennifer Rivas, a literacy coach in Texas, told us that "helping teachers go higher on Bloom's taxonomy" was a stated goal for coaches in her district. "At that moment, I felt the irony of only being familiar with Bloom's taxonomy at the 'Remember' level," she confided.

If you are a teacher, this will sound familiar. Maybe you have searched online for the pyramid displaying Bloom's taxonomy, or maybe you have dug out the Verb Wheel you picked up at a conference. You know how to write lessons promoting certain kinds of thinking by choosing the right verb to preface the lesson objectives. Ms. Rivas and

Ms. North both remarked that even after planning lessons with the right verbs, many teachers they know teach *hoping the verbs just happen.*

"Teaching thinking," in the Bloom's taxonomy sense, has been around for more than 40 years. And yet both national and international testing results show that today's students retain information well enough but fall short when asked to draw inferences about that information—when asked to really *think.* So, it's time to ask: *What if Bloom was wrong?*

Yes, we're going there.

Over the years, Bloom's taxonomy—and the pyramid poster depicting its hierarchical progression of thinking skills from knowledge to comprehension to application to analysis to synthesis to evaluation—has been a classroom staple. The revision made to the taxonomy (Anderson & Krathwohl, 2001) maintains the sequence: first remembering, then understanding, then applying, then analyzing, then evaluating, and then finally, creating. It's no wonder that many teachers assume tasks focused on lower-level skills like knowledge and application must be completed before tasks focused on higher-level skills, like synthesis or evaluation, can be undertaken. Bloom's taxonomy tells us that this is just how thinking works. But that isn't true.

According to neuroscientists who study brain imaging and interpret the brain's functions based on this research, thinking is not this linear. We process images, information, and interactions to detect and seek patterns; it is unlikely that we learn in a Bloom's-like progression, from lower- to higher-order thinking. Remembering is not necessarily the first step, and understanding is not the second. Research suggests that remembering and understanding can be, and often are, *the result* of applying, analyzing, and evaluating. These three skills help students remember and understand information to generate new and original ideas. The takeaway for teachers is that teaching students to apply, analyze, and evaluate better will help them to remember and understand—and generate ideas for themselves.

Then, there is this: If you return to the original book that Bloom edited (1956), you'll see that it does not actually propose a sequence of learning. The taxonomy, as presented, is an unfinished suggestion about a hierarchy of assessment options. So, maybe Bloom wasn't wrong; perhaps we were wrong in our interpretation.

The claim just presented, whether you agree with it or not, is an example of an argument with a concession. Writing argumentative essays is a staple in today's classroom, and many states require students to begin "writing" opinion pieces as early as kindergarten. Teaching students the steps to construct an argument is not just a key component of teaching thinking, it's a practical necessity to address in this information age.

Ask yourself: What kinds of **argument-construction tasks** do you assign, and for what purposes? Then, with these tasks in mind, ask yourself the **i5 questions**:

1. How else could the students and I search for *information?*
2. How else could we use visual *images* and nonlinguistic representations to add meaning?
3. How could I encourage students to *interact* with others, live or through social media, to obtain and provide feedback?
4. How could I teach the *inquiry* skill—argument—to deepen knowledge?
5. How could I plan for the students to use the application to generate *innovative* insights and products related to the lesson goals?

The Procedure

It is because students are likely to see an argumentative essay on an assessment—making a claim and then supporting it with evidence—that it's so important to teach this skill explicitly, regardless of grade level, so that the process students are following is a solid one.

Figure 4.2 shows the steps of constructing an argument.

FIGURE 4.2
How to Construct an Argument

The objective: Make a claim supported by evidence and examples.

Steps in the Process	Simplified Language
1. Describe an event or issue.	1. Tell about a situation.
2. Prepare and state a claim defending, refuting, or reflecting on the topic.	2. State your opinion about the situation.
3. Provide detailed evidence and elaboration about the claim.	3. Explain your opinion with examples.
4. Offer a counterclaim with support.	4. State an opposite opinion about the situation.
5. Summarize and use the findings to generate a new insight about the event or issue.	5. Tell what you know now or how to make the situation better.

In constructing an argument, there are two equally critical pivots that elevate the level of inquiry. The first is students' work to prepare and state a claim (Step 2). In this context, the claim is a new idea or an original insight that has emerged through the gathering and synthesizing of information. The second pivot is the counterclaim or concession (Step 4). Here, students must evaluate their idea, consider its flip side, and find something there deserving of support. It's the necessarily humbling recognition of other people's opinions.

In the Classroom: Lesson Examples

The Penal Colony

Natalie DeBrincat teaches a combined class of 5th and 6th graders in Melbourne, Australia. She admitted that the part of her curriculum focused on Australia's history as collection of British penal colonies always seemed to fall flat. Because of what she believed was sensitive subject matter, she felt obligated to explain as much as she could to her students; subsequently, she found herself *telling* more than teaching. Using the i5 approach, Ms. DeBrincat took a new tack: the lesson would focus on having students construct an argument for or against Britain's establishment of these penal colonies and the hundred-year practice of transporting convicts to the Australian continent and its surrounding islands.

Ms. DeBrincat was pleased and surprised to find lots of grade-appropriate resources related to the topic online, both *information* and *images*, as well as links describing social, political, and economic contexts critical to helping the students construct an argument for or against convict settlement (*inquiry*). Her students needed to gather lots of information before they could think deeply about it.

The lesson began with showing students two *images*: one, a black-and-white drawing depicting a London street of the 1700s, filled with people, carriages, and shops, and the other, a rendering of four barefoot indigenous children fishing by a pond with no one else around. Ms. DeBrincat asked students to list three things they noticed in each *image*. After some discussion, everyone agreed that one image was very crowded and one was not.

Next, the students read the articles from the sources online (*information*) using a jigsaw method and added notes to a common online organizer (*interaction*). Then Ms. DeBrincat explicitly taught the class the steps to constructing an argument, including identifying a counterargument. "That was when the debate really started," she proudly told us. As the students presented their claims with evidence (*innovation*), many who argued that the colonization was positive took the position that the policy added multiculturalism to the country. Others who argued that the effects of the policy were detrimental did so in support of the native groups who suffered because of the resettlement practices.

The i5 Reflection: Ms. DeBrincat was surprised by the direction the discussions took after she updated this lesson with the i5 approach. In previous years, her classes about Australia's history as a penal colony had focused on prisons and prisoners, but challenging students to do their own readings and make a claim based on what they read connected them with more complex and far-reaching societal concepts. Teaching inquiry skills had built deeper, more meaningful understandings—not just for the students but for their teacher as well. Moving forward, Ms. DeBrincat said, she would be deliberate about teaching thinking skills in her lessons.

Revenue, Cost, and Profit: The Oops Room

Hammond's Candies, a company based in Denver, Colorado, knows a little something about generating new ideas. Visit its factory and you'll find the "Oops Room," a place where its "damaged goods"—broken candy canes, cracked butterscotch pillows, caramel roll ends, and anything that doesn't make the quality cut—are brightly packaged and sold to throngs of thrifty customers (Hammond's Candies, 2011). The idea creator for the *Oops Bags of Candy* must have made a convincing argument that it would indeed be possible to sell the factory's below-standard products!

Rusty Bishop, who teaches high school math in Tennessee, introduced his students to his own version of an Oops Room via a lesson about solving, calculating, and discovering the characteristics of quadratic functions. The lesson grew out of concern that some students would learn to use the formula when it was packaged for them, but not realize that industries use it to solve problems in real life. He had been encouraged to use problem-based learning, but he had not found that approach very successful; the students often ended up spending time on presentations rather than really delving deeply into applying the math in real-life ways.

Mr. Bishop set his lesson goal and developed an inquiry-based activity: students would construct an argument for the most profitable production plan (*inquiry*), similar to the Oops Room example, by applying polynomial functions (linear and quadratic equations) to a retail product to show revenue, cost, and profit. Working together in small groups ("companies"), students used revenue equation software to graph (*images*) and predict what number of items produced would yield the most revenue (*interaction*). The companies were encouraged to manipulate the various values in order to achieve maximum profitability, and Mr. Bishop posted their work so others could see the variations. By setting up the task as an argument, the students had a goal that involved gaining a deep understanding of the content before they could make the claim about the most profitable scenario.

The students predicted revenue, cost, and profit at certain values (e.g., 50 units, 100 units, 150 units, and 200 units). Using the profit equation and an online graphing program, they predicted how many units had to be sold to gain the most profit possible (*information*). The software enabled them to input multiple changes in just a few strokes of the keyboard, and they drew from their results to understand the key characteristics of a quadratic function (the solutions [x-intercepts, y-intercept, and vertex]) and then explain how they reached their conclusion (*innovation*).

This, to Mr. Bishop, was truly problem-based learning. He had tried having students identify and solve their own real-world "problems," but he had not previously taught the steps to creating an argument. The online software and ability to view one another's work at various points helped students by providing encouragement throughout the project.

The i5 Reflection: Mr. Bishop's i5 epiphany came when he realized that he was assuming the students would know the steps to use thinking skills if he just provided the math. After teaching the class to use graphing software to support their claims in the arguments, he noted that the students sought ideas from other groups, bartering information to make their own calculations work better. He realized that students can find motivation in math when they are taught thinking skills and how to apply them to open-ended tasks.

Summary

In this chapter, we discussed investigation and argument construction, two synthesis-related thinking skills that teachers assign regularly but may not be teaching explicitly. Especially with access to the internet, students learning to synthesize information for a productive result will be able to use the skill over and over. Although a summary is reducing a source to a condensed format, it does not have the same power as synthesizing. A synthesis combines multiple sources systematically to produce a new view or version.

In this chapter, the flexibility of the i5 approach from a preschool class to visual arts to a high school math class, allows teachers to challenge students, but also guide their thinking. The preschool teacher realized that her students could use a thinking skill if she provided enough content. In the visual arts class, Mr. Korb grasped that all the i's are important, including the one his ambitious students had initially overlooked—*inquiry*.

In the next chapter, we examine another category of thinking skills, *analysis*, which gives students and teachers additional tools to use when presenting and engaging with content.

Teaching the Skills of Analysis

In his book *Why Don't Students Like School?* cognitive scientist Daniel T. Willingham writes, "The brain is not designed for thinking" (2009, p. 3). It's a startling statement, but less so as you read on. Willingham points out that thinking is slow, effortful, uncertain, and unreliable— so much so that the brain seems to have built bypasses around it. The brain, Willingham says, is ingeniously designed *to save us from having to think*. We automatize tasks. We rely on memory. We like to solve problems, but we do not like to work on problems that seem unsolvable. This, he explains, is why students who view schoolwork as too hard will not like school very much (p. 4). To teachers, this all rings true.

Willingham (2007) also writes that critical thinking cannot be taught, and with this, we heartily disagree. Both research and our personal perspectives, informed by years of working with teachers in schools, convince us that critical thinking can be taught very effectively. The classic example is Reuven Feuerstein (1980) and his Instructional Enrichment tactics, which focused on building academic skills and social resilience in all children, both disadvantaged and gifted, at the same time it helped them take steps toward becoming critical and creative thinkers.

Students can learn to identify similarities and differences, synthesize information and extract themes, examine the structure or pattern of something that merits discussion, and generate and test hypotheses. When they are given the opportunity to think deeply about topics in school, students become more efficient at generating creative ideas and evaluating the worth of the task and the accuracy of their own performances.

Why Teach Analysis?

If synthesis is a process of gathering information from multiple sources to extract a theme, then analysis is the nearly opposite. When you analyze, you systematically break a whole into smaller parts to reveal its existing interrelationships and use these insights as the foundation for new understanding.

Second to the word *compare*, *analyze* is probably the most commonly used term in curriculums. Topics we ask secondary students to analyze range from explaining how water resources affect communities to the way that theatrical productions have changed from Ancient Greece to today. In elementary schools, students analyze character actions in stories, how simple machines work, and if information found online is true or not. Students at all levels are asked to analyze how things work (systems), how people respond (perspectives), and how people would know if they are being led to believe something that is not true (fallacies).

Even though analyzing is common in curriculums, many teachers assign and assess its component skills—**analyzing perspectives, systems analysis**, and **analyzing for fallacy or error**—without ever explicitly teaching the steps involved. The teaching and use of these skills will be our focus in this chapter.

Analyzing Perspectives

In the 21st century, when the world is becoming a smaller place and communication across cultures and communities has increased, there is value in teaching students how to consider others' points of view and listen to and tolerate others' opinions.

In the 1800s, J. F. Herbart introduced a teaching schema that went on to be widely used in both Europe and the United States. Herbart believed that the more information a person could learn and retain, the more open that person would be to new ideas and cultures. The goal of instruction, he asserted, was to develop this openness, this appercep-tion. Herbart's goal was not advancing student achievement per se, but he sought to create a more tolerant society to advance world peace (Pol-lock, 2007). The Herbartian schema is the seminal basis for the GANAG schema described in Chapter 2, and it's clear how training students in the careful consideration of points of view to support tolerance and judicious decision making would serve them well today.

Ask yourself: What kinds of **perspective-analysis tasks** do you assign, and for what purposes? Then, with these tasks in mind, ask yourself the **i5 questions**:

1. How else could the students and I search for *information?*
2. How else could we use visual *images* and nonlinguistic rep-resentations to add meaning?
3. How could I encourage students to *interact* with others, live or through social media, to obtain and provide feedback?
4. How could I teach the *inquiry* skill—analyzing perspec-tives—to deepen knowledge?
5. How could I plan for the students to use the application to generate *innovative* insights and products related to the lesson goals?

The Procedure

The skill of analyzing perspectives has lots of applications inside and outside the classroom, and it has long been a staple of English, history, and social studies classes. We can teach students to analyze perspectives in all subjects so they can literally learn what others know about a topic and begin to consider potential consequences or applications of these different takes. Students have many opportunities in elementary literacy classes to consider different viewpoints, as many stories center around a situation, and characters respond differently. But it has a place in mathematics classes, too, as South Carolina teacher Megan McDermid demonstrated in a 4th grade multiplication unit. She taught her students various algorithms and then introduced the skill of analyzing perspectives to help them to see why different people would choose to use different algorithms.

Figure 5.1 shows the process of analyzing multiple perspectives or points of view.

FIGURE 5.1
How to Analyze Perspectives or Points of View

The objective: Consider multiple takes on an issue.

Steps in the Process	Simplified Language
1. Describe an event or issue.	1. Describe a situation.
2. State a viewpoint that is expressed, supported by logic and evidence.	2. Tell how one person sees it.
3. Explain other viewpoints expressed, referencing supporting logic and evidence.	3. Tell how a different person sees it.
4. Explain the strengths, weaknesses, and unique features of the different viewpoints.	4. Give your opinion about the differences.
5. Summarize and use the findings to generate a new insight about the event or issue.	5. Explain what you know now or how to make it better.

The pivot step in the process of analyzing perspectives that shifts the thinker's role from a recipient of others' knowledge to an active, forward-thinking participant is being able to explain the disadvantages and the auspicious elements of any perspective; the thinker has now positioned himself or herself to see that many events are understood differently by different people, and that is productive. With the unlimited access to information online, teachers have a greatly expanded opportunity to teach students the power of seeking others' viewpoints.

In the Classroom: Lesson Examples
Why Julian and His Brother Hid

Lunch was over. Julie Finney's 3rd graders each grabbed a Chromebook as they entered the classroom and logged into their Google Classroom. A cartoon (*image*) greeted them on their individual devices. It showed a man stranded on an island in the middle of the ocean and looking out over the water at another man, stranded in a boat. The man in the boat was yelling, "Land!" while the man on the island was yelling, "Boat!" Ms. Finney would use the cartoon to introduce analyzing perspectives, but first she wanted to give her students a chance to process the concept. She asked them to each post one comment about the cartoon (*interaction*). They were used to either sharing their thoughts through live pair/ sharing or via electronic polling that immediately shows results on a big screen. Then, the class began discussing the cartoon—specifically, what the characters were seeing and saying, and what they might be feeling. Then Ms. Finney introduced the steps for analyzing perspective (*inquiry*) because students would be applying it to their reading.

This thinking skill activity was undertaken for a specific reason: Ms. Finney wanted her students to better understand how characters' actions contributed to the sequence of events in the book they were reading: *The Stories Julian Tells* (1981) by Ann Cameron. For example, in one chapter, Julian and his little brother eat an entire lemon pudding while their father naps. When the father wakes and discovers the pudding is gone, he announces there is going to be some whipping and beating! The play on words—that making a replacement pudding would involve vigorous application of the *kitchen skills* whipping and beating—is not obvious to Julian and his brother, nor was it obvious, at first, to many of Ms. Finney's students. To reinforce the multiple meanings of *whipping* and *beating,* she linked two cooking demonstration videos to the Google Classroom, giving her students an opportunity to see the culinary version of the verbs in action. She also linked a recipe for lemon pudding to add meaning (*information, images*).

Watching the video and looking at the images helped students better understand the vocabulary—a characteristic of "close reading." Then they worked through the steps of the thinking skill, which helped them make inferences throughout the rest of the text and generate their own thoughts (*innovation*), including that there are two or more sides to every situation.

The i5 Reflection: Two changes happened in Ms. Finney's class. First, she became aware that access to visuals and live interaction helped many students stay engaged in both understanding the text and the discussion. Second, the inquiry aspect of the i5 motivated her to make the class discussion focus more on the text itself. When analyzing perspectives, her students had to show where in the text the statement came from or how they inferred the viewpoint. Using inquiry made the "close reading" more robust by prompting the students to seek information and not just respond to the teacher's questions.

The Invention of Teenagers

Matthew Keiser told us that when he first started teaching, he was convinced that he needed to pack each lecture with as much information as he possibly could. After all, he reasoned, the students would need to apply the information for homework. Like most teachers, Mr. Keiser struggled with students not turning in assignments and losing interest during his teaching. Although he wanted to foster critical thinking in his classroom, he wasn't actually *teaching* critical thinking. "Nobody had ever suggested to me that I should actually teach students *how to engage in inquiry,*" he said. "I wanted my students to mature from rote thinkers to imaginative, innovative thinkers, but I realize now that I didn't give them the tools to do so, and my decision to assign that part of the learning as homework did not help matters." He became interested in how the i5 and teaching thinking would work in his class.

Mr. Keiser began with a trip back in time in his psychology class. Projected on a screen were a series of black-and-white *images*. A family with a half-dozen children on a farm in the late 1800s. Children working in a coal mine at the turn of the 20th century. Soldiers in World War I. The iconic image of a group of young people squashed into a phone booth in the 1950s. Mr. Keiser asked his students to pair up to draft a short list describing the changes in what appeared to be the responsibilities of adolescents over the past 100 years, based on photographs they'd seen. In the past, Mr. Keiser told us, he might have started this lesson simply by asking his students to define *teenager* and accepting a few comments, most of them humorous.

In this revamped version of the lesson, the students fired up their tablets and entered their thoughts into a shared document. As the list grew, conversations became more animated. Mr. Keiser posted the learning goal related to the adolescent life span development standard: *Describe the development of reasoning and morality.*

Mr. Keiser had found an interesting video to show called "The Invention of the Teenager" (The Independence Hall Association, n.d.), which argued that over the course of 100 years, young people between the ages of 13 and 19 had gone from being considered children to being mini-adults to becoming a whole new, in-between thing: teenagers (*images, information*). Students watched the video, took notes, and discussed the issue of how young adults today might develop morality differently from previous generations. Next, Mr. Keiser asked students to form pairs (*interaction*) to discuss a series of vignettes in which people had to make moral decisions about topics ranging from online behaviors to instances of theft or job expectations. The students' task was to view each situation from the point of view of a teenager in different decades.

He provided students with a curated list of starting points for their upcoming exploration of teenage-hood: websites and online collections of articles and images covering research findings on adolescent development and culture in the 20th and 21st centuries (*information, interaction*).

The students would be able to consider each vignette by inferring the viewpoints of teenagers in the different decades. They could analyze perspectives based on the online source information.

Students posted their analyses on the class website in a blog format so others could see the varied perspectives being gathered (*interaction*). To summarize, the students made predictions about what might change for young adults in the coming years, given the enormous and still evolving effect of modern communication and medical technology.

The i5 Reflection: "Who Invented Teenagers?" was the first lesson Mr. Keiser designed with the i5 approach. It was part of a unit on adolescence, and, he told us, he once delivered it simply by lecturing; then, he led a discussion in which he did most of the talking.

Mr. Keiser's approach today is very different from what it once was. He's prepared to lecture but also to teach students to gather information themselves via the technology that's available. Encouraging students to work together now is critical to process the vast amounts of information because once they find new sources, they have lots of clarifying questions. He says that teaching the thinking skill gives him valuable footholds in conversations—ways he can both guide and cue students to make inferences or seek more information.

Analyzing Systems

What happens when you change one part of a whole? For example, when presented with a math problem, what if you multiply rather than add? What if Britain were not limited by its own geographical boundaries but could expand to nonadjacent boundaries? What if we are not alone in the universe? Each of these inquiries provides an opportunity to take something apart—the numbers, the nation, the cosmos—to more deeply understand how that something works, what it produces, or how it could be improved. This is systems analysis, otherwise known as determining how the whole is affected by one or more of its parts, and it is one of the most flexible inquiry techniques because its results are usually creative as well as critical.

Systems analysis is a powerful tool for asking "what if?" questions. It's an opportunity to frame all kinds of subject matter—an epoch, an event, an organization, a type of technology, an experiment, or even a story or poem—as a system that could be changed in any number of ways to produce different results.

Ask yourself: What kinds of **systems-analysis tasks** do you assign, and for what purposes? Then, with these tasks in mind, ask yourself the **i5 questions**:

1. How else could the students and I search for *information?*
2. How else could we use visual *images* and nonlinguistic representations to add meaning?
3. How could I encourage students to *interact* with others, live or through social media, to obtain and provide feedback?
4. How could I teach the *inquiry* skill—analyzing systems—to deepen knowledge?
5. How could I plan for the students to use the application to generate *innovative* insights and products related to the lesson goals?

The Procedure

Wondering—asking "what if?"—comes naturally to many. But all students need to be aware that this kind of curiosity can be focused into a practical tool, and they need to be taught how to wield it.

Much time in classrooms is spent ensuring that students learn the parts and functions of the whole of a topic, but we tend not to spend too much time on making changes or exploring errors. This may be why, in real life, more of us call in experts to explain or deal with systems that go awry than spend time researching DIY fixes to leaking faucets, computer problems, nagging back pain, or any number of other obstacles. No, of course, we cannot teach all aspects of every system, but we can give students practice viewing something as a system and learning to anticipate how changes affect that system's functions and results. Figure 5.2 shows the steps in the inquiry skill of systems analysis.

FIGURE 5.2
How to Analyze a System

The objective: Know how the parts of a system impact the whole.

Steps in the Process	Simplified Language
1. Identify an object, event, or thing as a system.	1. Name something you will think about as a system.
2. Describe its parts and how they function.	2. Tell how the parts of it work.
3. Change a part or function and explain how it affects the whole.	3. Change one part and tell how the whole thing works now.
4. Change another part and explain the results. (This step can be repeated multiple times.)	4. Do it again with a different part.
5. Summarize and use the findings to generate deeper understanding or an improvement to the system.	5. Explain what you know now about the thing or how to make it better.

In this thinking skill, the pivot step is Step 3, the changing step. What happens when you add or delete a part? If you vary a practice or procedure in some way? For a student making a table in a carpentry class, varying the height or width of the tabletop may prove to be useful. For a student creating a movie in a science class, offering the conclusion of the experiment at the beginning may provide a more engaging product for the audience. Change can lead to productive ends.

Truth be told, systems analysis is fun to teach. Students love to consider "What would happen if...?" questions. *What would happen if the character in the novel made a different decision? If the animal had access to a shelter? If the road veered off in a different direction? If the colors were reversed? If the rules of the game allowed a player to do something else?* Answering these kinds of questions involves speculating based on what you already know. Systems analysis may sound static, yet it is one of the most creative processes human beings have at our disposal, and it's a powerful tool we can use to understand the world around us and figure out how to make it better.

In the Classroom: Lesson Examples

Limericks

The 4th grade language arts curriculum's coverage of poetry includes teaching limericks, those short, silly poems that use puns and wordplay to entertain. When Trisha Grayson, the teacher, and Deborah Goff, the literacy coach, started a limericks lessons, they thought it would be simple: teach the structure (five lines following an AABBA rhyme scheme), read a few limericks to the class, and ask students to produce their own. They were surprised to find that many students struggled and needed a lot of teacher help but still did not generate very good product. Ms. Grayson and Ms. Goff turned to the i5 approach.

Beginning with *information,* they searched online and found a wealth of historical data on Edward Lear (remembered for "The Owl and the Pussy-cat") and several of his limericks, which make fun of the stuffiness of the Victorian era. Here's one from Lear's 1846 publication, *A Book of Nonsense*:

> There was an Old Man with a beard,
> Who said, "It is just as I feared!
> Two Owls and a Hen,
> Four Larks and a Wren,
> Have all built their nests in my beard!"

As the teachers searched for "kid limericks" or "funny limericks," they found that searching for *images* instead of words resulted in much better examples. Online, numerous limericks were shown with clip art that boosted the students' understanding of many of the terms. Pairing students together for *interaction* was important in this lesson because limericks tend to use dry humor; students needed to clarify vocabulary to understand the puns.

The teachers chose to teach the students to use systems analysis because they remembered the previous struggles with the rhyming structure, even though it looks very simple. Following the steps, students started off by changing one word to see if the limerick still adhered to the rhyming pattern; this helped clarify the importance of the form's structure. After making multiple experimental changes and discussing the repercussions, the students had the opportunity to write their own limericks (*innovation*). Now the students got it! They were able to create limericks and generate their own visuals like the ones they saw online.

The i5 Reflection: The i5 was integral to motivating the teachers to provide students with more information about limericks as they approached the task. In previous years, when they delivered the lesson by presenting one or two sample limericks, students didn't have enough material to think about. Asking students to use technology to search for multiple examples helped them understand this form of poetry. In addition, teaching the inquiry skill of systems analysis and framing the limerick form as a system allowed students to more fully comprehend the form's structure and rhyming pattern, improving their ability to generate their own limericks.

Grandma's Eyes

Art teacher Lauren McCalman's portraiture unit for her middle school class teaches students to draw portraits by focusing on different facial parts, and drawing realistic eyes is the focus of the first two days of the unit.

When students entered the art room on the day of the lesson, streaming on the screen at the front of the room was a short clip from the movie *Into the Woods*, showing the character of Little Red (Riding

Hood) meeting up with Mr. Wolf. Even those who hadn't seen the movie before recognized what was about to happen—that the little girl in the red cape would eventually get around to pronouncing, "But Grandma, what great big eyes you have!"

In their sketchbooks, students responded to Ms. McCalman's cue to draw a pair of great big eyes and, when prompted, shared their sketches with their table partners. Ms. McCalman drew a couple of great big clownish eyes on the board, and most students snickered that they looked like their own drawings: too round, missing eyelashes, and with irises that are too dark.

At this point, Ms. McCalman shared the learning goal for this lesson: to draw a realistic eye. Students copied the goal into their notebooks and self-assessed this "before" sketch using a simple scale: 1—"Good enough for the fridge"; 2—"Good enough for a friend"; 3—"Good enough to publish"; 4—"Good enough for a gallery." Ms. McCalman walked around to check on students' scores.

Ms. McCalman then projected an original seven-minute video that illustrated nine steps to drawing a realistic eye (*information, images*). The students took notes, and she paused the video intermittently to check for understanding. With this procedural knowledge fresh in their minds, students drew a second eye and compared it to their first, sharing the comparisons with peers at their tables. Generally, the drawings were better, but they were still not quite as good as some of the images found online. Ms. McCalman assured the class that they would get a third chance to draw.

At this point, she introduced the thinking skill of systems analysis (*inquiry*), projecting a copy of the procedure's steps she had adapted to reflect the specific challenge ahead:

Systems Analysis
1. Visualize an eye as a system.
2. Describe the nine parts of the illustrated eye.
3. Select one (or more) part(s) of the eye and change it, draw the result, and explain how the change affects the sketch.

4. Repeat Step 3.

5. Generate a new sketch.

Ms. McCalman then modeled this procedure, drawing an eye on the board. On reaching Step 3 of the systems analysis procedure, she announced that the change she was going to make would be to leave out the shading near the lashes. She did… and stepped back and scrutinized the work. Thinking aloud, she mused that without the shading, the eye looked too round. "Too round!" she wrote next to her sketch. She went on to draw various eyes, each time skipping a different step in the drawing procedure and then critiquing the result. (Ms. McCalman told us that learning about teaching the thinking skill influenced her techniques for this part of the lesson. In the past, she would sketch the eye on the board and give students a handout with the nine steps. Students would then work on their own for the rest of the class period, and she would walk around helping students and then collecting their sketches when the bell rang.)

The next phase of the lessons involved students pairing up and drawing an eye at least five more times, omitting one or more of the nine procedural steps and adding a description or critique of the results next to the sketch. Students posted their work on the shared drive so it was accessible to the whole class via digital devices to critique (*interaction*). Students sketched quickly, interacting with one another and some extended the skill by making pairs of changes to see the outcomes. In just five or six minutes, the students had become comfortable acting as both critical viewers and experts in the context of drawing realistic eyes. As Ms. McCalman later told us, their engagement came not from trying to get the eyes "right," but because the open-ended analysis task was like a puzzle for them to solve. Some of the results encouraged students to try to get results that showed emotion by changing parts deliberately. "The buzz in the room was different," Ms. McCalman said. "The students were asking me to come see their work—not to come help them with it."

With 10 minutes left to finish the lesson, Ms. McCalman asked the class to turn to a clean page in their sketchbooks, explaining that they would have two minutes to draw a pair of eyes. At the end of the two minutes, students uploaded both their "before" (pre-instruction) sketch and their "after" sketch to the class website for all to see. "Score yourself," Ms. McCalman, reminded them. "Are your eyes ready for the fridge, or ready for the gallery?"

As the students prepared to leave, one asked, "Will we do this systems analysis for the other parts of the face, too? It helped me remember to do all of the steps when it came to the last sketch." Ms. McCalman affirmed that they would. It's an approach that works.

The i5 Reflection: Ms. McCalman admitted that when she was first introduced to the idea of explicitly teaching thinking skills, she was skeptical about its usefulness for teachers like herself, who taught in a workshop classroom. "I was wrong!" she laughed.

Then she opened the online portfolio for the class, showing dozens of remarkably realistic eyes, from dreamy, heavy-lidded pairs to brighter, doe-eyed ones. "I want to tell you about the transformation in my students' products," she said, "because last year, honestly only a few of the 'after' pictures looked like these. This year, every student showed unusual ability to improve upon their initial sketches." The difference, Ms. McCalman told us, was the way that the i5 approach guided her to incorporate technology—to facilitate engagement, and, more significantly, to teach not just the procedural steps to drawing an eye but also the inquiry skill that focused students on the work and seemed to empower their progress. To her, the biggest surprise from using the i5 to add teaching the thinking skill of systems analysis was the way it increased student engagement and added complexity to their results.

Finding Error

There is a clever PDF available online depicting images of Socrates, Plato, and Aristotle above the proclamation "Thou shalt not commit logical fallacies." The philosophers are surrounded by descriptions of common logical fallacies: strawman, slippery slope, loaded questions, begging the question, and the bandwagon appeal. (This PDF is free and can be downloaded from https://yourlogicalfallacyis.com/poster.) Anyone who was on the debate team at school can rattle off phrases like *ad hominem* and *tu quoque* in an attempt to appeal to authority and make themselves sound savvier than the rest of us. But being able to find errors in reasoning should be a skill taught to every student, especially in the age of the internet. The ability to read and listen critically and figure out what someone is trying to get you to believe through means such as rhetoric or emotional manipulation provides students with a lifelong tool for processing information received from various sources.

Ask yourself: What kinds of **error-finding tasks** do you assign, and for what purposes? Then, with these tasks in mind, ask yourself the **i5 questions**:

1. How else could the students and I search for *information?*
2. How else could we use visual *images* and nonlinguistic representations to add meaning?
3. How could I encourage students to *interact* with others, live or through social media, to obtain and provide feedback?
4. How could I teach the *inquiry* skill—finding error—to deepen knowledge?
5. How could I plan for the students to use the application to generate *innovative* insights and products related to the lesson goals?

The Procedure

One reality of the digital age is that students will be reading and listening to a lot of unfiltered information. Accordingly, a critical skill for these voracious consumers of information to develop is the ability to discern what the content's creator is trying to persuade them to believe and to determine the soundness the argument presented.

If you search online for "errors in reasoning" or "logical fallacy," you'll find various lists of some of the more common examples, such as a non-sequitur (asserting a conclusion that cannot be drawn from the facts) or a red herring (using a reference to distract from the argument). Students can learn to find the errors in readings online as a way to be more confident about their knowledge. Teaching the inquiry skill of finding error is a way to empower students to evaluate the arguments they encounter while doing research, encountering new information, and interacting in online spaces. Figure 5.3 shows the steps.

FIGURE 5.3
How to Find Errors in Reasoning

The objective: Recognize errors in thinking.

Steps in the Process	Simplified Language
1. Describe an event, situation, or argument that is presented to you.	1. Tell about a situation or opinion.
2. Identify the tactics (fallacies) used to manipulate the truth.	2. Say what the presenter is trying to get you to believe.
3. Explain possible misunderstandings based on the error in reasoning.	3. Explain what might not be true.
4. Summarize and use findings to generate a new idea or product.	4. Explain what you believe to be true.

Sometimes logical fallacies are hard to see, and this is especially true when you are in general agreement with the argument. The pivotal step in this thinking skill is the ability to explain the misunderstanding. The author may appeal to an authority, for example, but it is important to see both sides of the story—why the appeal works for those in favor but also why it does not work for those who are not in favor.

In the Classroom: Lesson Examples
Digital Anonymity

There is a particular quotation that keeps elementary school technology teacher George Santos up at night. It is this statement from Kevin Honeycutt, a speaker on technology, education, and cyberbullying prevention: "Our kids are growing up on a digital playground, and no one is on recess duty."

Among the topics that Sr. Santos teaches his students is online identity impersonation and internet safety. Considering the i5 approach prompted him to remark that he already did a good job incorporating information and images into his instruction, but he was pretty sure that any interaction his lessons afforded students was not deliberate and that he might not be explicitly teaching the thinking skills students needed. He set out to change this.

Sr. Santos opened a lesson on digital anonymity by showing a video of a police sketch artist at work. He pointed out how the sketch artist drew the characteristics of a person as they were described to him in detail (*information, images*). Next, he told the students that he was going to let them be sketch artists, but they would be drawing people speaking rather than people being described. He would play audio clips, and they would need to listen very carefully to each. "I would like you to listen to the sound of each speaker's voice and vocal inflections, listen to what the speaker is talking about, and then draw a picture of the speaker based on how he or she sounds."

Students worked in groups of three to listen, discuss, and draw. They made a quick collective sketch of each person speaking and wrote a few phrases of description (*interaction*) until they had sketched a half-dozen different characters ranging from a kindly elderly lady to a brash and cocky young athlete.

Sr. Santos presented and modeled the steps for finding errors in reasoning, and then he asked his students to apply the skill as they listened to the audio clips a second time (*inquiry*). He stressed that they should focus, in each case, on how the speaker was revealing his or her personality through the topics discussed. "Listen to what's being said," he advised. "Note *how* it's being said. See if you can identify specific tactics that are being used to influence your interpretation of who is speaking." After the replays, students in the small groups reviewed the notes they'd taken, discussed how the person's voice and the detail influenced their idea of what the person looked like and shared these thoughts with the rest of the class. Then Sr. Santos played the video that showed the six speakers. To the students' amazement, it was just one person—an impersonator putting on all the voices.

In the ensuing discussion, Sr. Santos's students commented that the task had driven home how risky it can be to believe that strangers they meet online and via texts or other electronic communication really are who they say they are. To complete the lesson, students devised their own personal responsibility and commitment statements addressing digital anonymity (*innovation*). They shared their statements on the class website, which is accessible to parents and other teachers.

The i5 Reflection: Sr. Santos noted that the i5 stretched his repertoire not in the technology arena, but in the way in which it encouraged students to use inquiry skills. In the past, he would have lectured to the students about the risks of believing that the people online are who they claim to be. The i5 approach, he noted, resulted in a more effective lesson and motivated him to reconsider other lessons in which the students would read online blogs to find other examples where the author used fallacious reasoning to make arguments.

Too Many Books About the Holocaust?

Jennifer Rivas, a literacy coach, and Lorena Pasos, an 8th grade English teacher, decided to apply the i5 approach to teach students to find error in reasoning in the context of their unit on the Holocaust. In previous units, students had learned to use rhetorical devices to support their persuasive arguments. Now students would uncover those devices in a text.

The teachers started off with some playacting. As the 8th graders entered the classroom, settled into their seats, and began copying the lesson's goal (*Determine an author's point of view, and analyze how the author responds to conflicting viewpoints*) into their notebooks, Ms. Rivas exclaimed to Ms. Pasos, "There are just too many books about the Holocaust these days." Ms. Pasos nodded enthusiastically and added, "Yes, and too many movies about the Holocaust as well."

Most of the students kept writing while simultaneously eavesdropping on the teachers' discussion of whether society had reached a saturation point with Holocaust books and movies. One student raised her hand and blurted out before being called on, "Ms. Pasos, didn't you like the movie about the book thief who was really the girl who did the laundry, but read all of the books?" Then another student jumped in with, "What about the one where the two boys are friends, and the fence is between them?" It does not take much to prime 13-year-olds.

Ms. Pasos turned to address the whole class. "For the past two weeks, we've been reading and analyzing excerpts online from three books about the Holocaust, and we watched the video that presented real photos and documents from World War II (*information, images*). Now, Ms. Rivas and I are going to ask you to evaluate the position the author takes in this article." This was Ms. Rivas's cue to project a blog post titled "Are There Too Many Books About the Holocaust?"

Ms. Rivas then projected and reviewed the steps to the skill of finding error in reasoning (*inquiry*) and explained that that task ahead would involve analyzing the text for logical fallacy—statements where the writer made an error in reasoning, manipulated the content, or used a rhetorical device (such as begging the question or appealing to authority) to advance the argument. For homework, students could access responses to the blog as well as other similar articles and join a class conversation about whether the author had convinced them (*interaction*).

During the class discussion, students sat in two groups: "the convinced," and "the unconvinced." Everyone had an opportunity to explain why and how the author had or had not convinced them, citing specific instances of fallacies and rhetorical devices within the text. As a wrap up, each student wrote a short response (50 words or less) to the blog post and shared it on the class site. It seemed that the "convinced" side dwindled as the exploration went on, and students' written responses were filled with references to the fact that more exposure to stories and novels like these could only improve understanding and tolerance.

The i5 Reflection: Both teachers agreed that following the i5 approach encouraged them to try something new. They had shown video and images and assigned articles on the Holocaust and its lasting impact, but they had never explicitly taught a thinking skill that would support this kind of analytical discussion of the topic. Reading for errors in reasoning provided the right level of challenge to engage their students to seek more articles to see the level of credibility of the source.

Summary

In school and in life, students will encounter many situations that require them to stop and think. Learning to analyze perspectives, deliberately examine a situation as a system, and assess information for errors in reasoning will give students tools to methodically evaluate information for accuracy and value, leading to deeper understanding of the material.

From our past experiences, it seems that many teachers believe thinking skill development is something that takes place only when students are involved in projects. That is not the case. Most lessons lend themselves quite readily to short, 10- to 15-minute periods of knowledge application, when the students can practice using thinking skills to consider different relationships, as in analysis. Once the students learn to use the various thinking skills with ease, they are more adept at applying them to more deeply understand content, parsing and deconstructing information on the way to generating new, innovative takes on it.

Consider, too, that in our digital world, students can and should learn to think carefully and productively about the internet's seemingly unlimited content. When following the i5 approach, keep in mind that students can more easily connect with the material when the lesson incorporates contexts or situations that are relevant to them. In each of the examples in this chapter, teachers created relevant problems that helped their students learn valuable content and develop essential critical thinking skills.

Teaching the Skills of Taking Action

John Ratey has a mission. The psychiatrist travels the world to tell people, especially school leaders, that exercise makes the brain better, and that it's a mistake to cut physical education classes from the curriculum if learning is the objective. In fact, Ratey recommends that all students take PE every day. In his book *Spark* (2008), he writes about studies that have shown that "exercise spawns neurons, and the stimulation of environmental enrichment helps those cells survive" (p. 49). Movement has a deep impact on how people learn; the more neurons you have, the more you can learn. Ratey cites data that show that students who participated in PE classes performed better on academic tests. According to neuroscience, we need brain cells to grow if we want to learn, and movement stimulates neurogenesis.

In *Spark*, Ratey explains that studies show that physical activity not only is an agent of neurogenesis, but it also helps us to regulate emotion. He writes, "I want to cement the idea that exercise has a profound impact on cognitive abilities and mental health. It is simply one of the best treatments we have for most psychiatric problems" (2008, p. 7). To his patients, he enthusiastically recommends exercise, even walking, over pharmaceuticals to mediate depression and other conditions, and he claims astounding results.

Ratey and his fellow scientists stand as a model for how to take action. Through study, they identify situations that need solutions, and they perform tests, make decisions, and generate new protocols. The prerequisite for action is knowledge; when we know about a topic, we can act to improve any situation.

Why Teach Taking Action?

Norman Doidge, a psychiatrist, writes about neuroplasticity because he is enthusiastic about the newer research— the fact that the brain can change, adapt, and grow throughout life. For thousands of years, scientists believed that the brain was rigid and inflexible with localized memory; today, they believe that making memories is dynamic. The brain can transform, compensate, and generate new neurons. When specifically discussing the executive functions of the frontal lobes, Doidge describes them as vibrant and able to "focus on goals, extract themes from what we perceive, and make decisions" (2007, p. 90). He and others point out that because the prefrontal cortex plays such a central role in goal formation, it also takes on the task of devising plans of actions required to attain the goals and evaluates progress toward these goals.

The kinds of inquiry addressed in this chapter are ones identified as the "Taking Action" skills. These are the strategies we use to generate and test ideas or options as they relate to information that we receive, process, and store. In *Classroom Instruction That Works* (Marzano et al., 2001), Jane and her colleagues identified the strategy of generating and testing hypotheses as having a high probability of increasing student learning ($d = 0.61$).

Taking action usually begins with a situation or event. If the event involves obstacles, we try to solve the problem; if it provides alternatives, we choose from among them; if the event allows the conditions, we test it; if it generates a need, we set the standards and create the item. In this category of thinking skills, the new idea is the solution, best choice, conclusion, and product.

This chapter explains how to teach students the essential skills related to taking action with knowledge they acquire—what they can do to solve, decide, test, and create.

Solving

On most days, facing unexpected obstacles is just something we expect. Problems can range from small and quickly solved to complex and requiring more information and effort. Say you're about to mow your lawn and you realize the mower blade is bent. What can you do? Well, you could use a different mower, maybe borrowing one from a neighbor; you could put off the chore; you could fix the blade now; and so on. You consider the situation, hypothesize possible solutions, and apply one. The more solutions that you generate, the more likely a good option will emerge. Problem solving depends on being able to devise lots of possible solutions and then making a considered choice. Generally, the more you know about the situation, the more likely you will be able to generate useful options for solving it. And although the problems students tend to see in class are often quite structured—especially in math class, where "solve" and "apply the formula" can too often be interpreted as synonyms—real life is messy. Students can learn to solve those problems, too.

The Procedure

Being able to follow a set of steps when approaching an unstructured problem will take you a considerable way toward a reasonable and satisfactory solution. Most of the school examples of solving tasks we see focus students almost exclusively on the language of the problem— on defining what the problem is asking them to do. However, the pivotal thinking step in solving is not defining the problem, but generating multiple solutions from which to choose. The late Stephen Covey (2011) reminded us to always look for "the 3rd alternative," meaning that when problems arise, one ought to push the limits and seek out unusual and unique solutions. That phrase should be a staple in every classroom.

Ask yourself: What kinds of **solving tasks** do you assign, and for what purposes? Then, with these tasks in mind, ask yourself the **i5 questions**:

1. How else could the students and I search for *information?*
2. How else could we use visual *images* and nonlinguistic representations to add meaning?
3. How could I encourage students to *interact* with others, live or through social media, to obtain and provide feedback?
4. How could I teach the *inquiry* skill—solving—to deepen knowledge?
5. How could I plan for the students to use the application to generate *innovative* insights and products related to the lesson goals?

Figure 6.1 shows the steps of solving to teach to and develop in students.

Identifying multiple solutions to meet the goal is the passive-to-active part of this thinking skill. Let's try it out here. Four teachers from the same elementary school are out of the building attending a professional development session, and only three substitute teachers show up. The principal begins to hypothesize possible solutions for supervising the students in the fourth class. Will she forgo her regular duties and cover the class herself? Divide the students into groups and parcel them out to other classrooms? Ask a parent volunteer to step in? Call one teacher and ask her to return to school and miss the training? Because each problem we encounter is unique, we cannot expect there to always be a checklist or a protocol specifically designed to tell us what to do; we must be prepared to *solve* problems. The solution chosen is the new idea—generated through the process of organizing and reorganizing our thoughts and ideas.

FIGURE 6.1
How to Solve

The objective: Navigate obstacles to find a good solution to a problem.

Steps in the Process	Simplified Language
1. Describe a situation that involves a goal.	1. Identify a goal.
2. Explain a barrier or barriers that prevent accomplishing the goal.	2. Explain something that gets in the way of reaching the goal.
3. Identify multiple solutions to meet the goal.	3. Identify a few ways to solve the problem.
4. Try a solution to overcome the barrier.	4. Try one of the ways to see how it works.
5. Repeat with other solutions.	5. Try another way.
6. Explain which solution you will use and how you will take action.	6. Use what you learned to take action.

In the Classroom: Lesson Examples

Solving the David Stories

Literature is a great way to teach students to solve problems that life presents, and the David stories by David Shannon are no exception. The books *No, David!* (1998), *David Goes to School* (1999), and *David Gets in Trouble* (2002) provide many opportunities for younger students to identify a problem (chewing with one's mouth open, tracking mud on the carpet) and think through multiple solutions. Bethany Moore said that she always loved reading these stories to her 1st graders, but our conversation about thinking skills helped her realize that they were a great context for teaching 1st graders how to solve problems.

Ms. Moore chose the three David stories mentioned to apply the problem-solving skill (*inquiry*). She regularly uses the online version of a book to read, projecting it on a large screen that all students can see from their seats, and she pauses the video to have students discuss it in pairs (*information, images, interaction*). Later, they can read and listen to the books in centers on their digital devices.

To teach problem solving, Ms. Moore modeled the steps to the process with two of the David books and led a discussion of the problems and solutions that included pair discussions with shoulder partners (*interaction*). Then she used an organizer listing the steps to walk students through identifying the problem and generating possible solutions. To wrap up the thinking skill, students identified the solution that would work best—that was "the new idea" (*innovation*).

After this modeling activity, Ms. Moore's students were eager to try it out on their own, so she invited them to use the third book and repeat the solving procedure on their own, individually. They also asked to try to solve problems in books written by other authors.

The i5 Reflection: Ms. Moore noted that the i5 approach may have had more of an impact on her planning than she had thought. She said the i5 changed the way she discussed stories with her students, because the interactions became guided by the thinking the class was doing, not just the story narrative. In the past, she had become accustomed to asking a question and being happy to have one student answer; now, problem solving with the steps taught her to expect more responses and to press students to generate solutions rather than just comment about the text. The methodical aspect of the inquiry skill encouraged her not to just accept any answer but to prod the issues before moving on. As soon as Ms. Moore started to plan for the David stories, she realized how many other books and author videos were available online—and how useful the approach she'd taken in this lesson would be for future lessons. She could turn to it for all kinds of reading and effectively tailor the activity to the different interests and developmental levels of the various students in her class.

Explicit Instruction—Even in Math

Middle school math teachers Robert Hammer and Steve Fougere teamed up to solve a shared problem: How could they raise their students' test scores? Their solution was to change the way they taught math at their respective schools, near Halifax, Nova Scotia. They began considering how to include explicit thinking skills instruction in their classes.

One of their first decisions, they told us, was they could probably skip instruction in the skill of problem solving; as math teachers, they figured they already devoted plenty of time to it. In fact, they had created a "tool chest for problem solving" that their students referenced all of the time—21 strategies that ranged from using measuring devices to drawing a diagram. When students were stuck, the teachers explained, they would suggest one of the 21 strategies, and the students would apply it and get back on track. It was at this moment, while Mr. Hammer and Mr. Fougere were discussing why they didn't need to teach problem solving, that they had their i5 epiphany. They had set up a system where *they* were the ones offering students the solution strategy, and therefore, *they*—and not their students—were the ones doing the thinking. Back to the drawing board, they said (*inquiry*).

Mr. Hammer and Mr. Fougere pared their set of 21 tools down to the six most useful strategies for solving the kinds of math problems included in their curriculum:

1. Generate a table and graph it or identify a pattern.
2. Use algebra to create an equation.
3. Draw a diagram.
4. Work backward, or try an easier problem of the same nature.
5. Use logical reasoning.
6. Use a formula or apply a set of rules.

They used a real-life example to introduce this revised tool chest: a simple analogy about crossing a mountain. *How does a person cross a mountain?* they asked, and then used images to illustrate the various strategies available—go through a tunnel, climb over the mountain range, go down to the valley below in a boat and row and portage over land. Next, they presented various math problems and described how each could be solved using any of the six math strategies. They also posted these solutions online so that their students would have access to them and to links related to them (*information, images*).

When the time came to decide how to generate a solution (Step 3 in the process), they modeled each strategy's application, and then invited students to choose a strategy and explain in small groups why it would or would not work (*inquiry, interaction*). The teachers went on to add a new section to the class electronic portfolio that included these six strategies, along with student-created examples to model application. Mr. Hammer and Mr. Fougere continued to model various problem-solving strategies in class for several days, guided their students to practice using different strategies for different problems, and encouraged them to bookmark good websites to use as sources for graphs, explanations, and formulas (*information, images*).

Often, students would state that they tried one strategy and got an answer, but they wanted to try a second to see if they got the same solution. In this way, they learned to generate multiple views of the same problem (*inquiry*). Occasionally the teachers assigned the math lesson as a flipped class, so that they could maximize observation time, see how the students were solving problems, and give them lots of feedback. In a short period of time, both teachers' students became more independent and more adept helping one another work through problems. For many of the students, online access to the tools helped them when they finished problems at home.

The i5 Reflection: Both teachers admitted that they were surprised to realize they had been doing too much thinking for their students. Once they taught problem solving as a thinking skill, students were more likely to go online to find more examples or information, to use graphing and diagramming programs, and to keep the electronic portfolio up to date. Students improved in both their academics and their motivation to try problems on their own using the tools in the digital toolbox.

Decision Making

Abby Sofia must make a decision. Looking at the high school schedule on her iPad, she sees that if she signs up for the history class, she won't be able to take a second science class. She's a junior, so she still has a chance next year to double up on science, and she can take Mandarin for a second year, too. She sends a text to her friend Maxie to see what she knows about the history class. Racing out of her bedroom, Abby Sofia almost steps on her younger brother, John Diego, who is lying on the floor in the hallway sorting Pokémon cards and muttering to himself about one card being a better trade than the other because of the traits listed below the picture. Abby Sofia ruffles her brother's hair, reminding him to put the cards away until after school. "Made up my mind," he says. "I'm going to trade Tentacruel!" Dad calls out to them to hurry up to catch the bus.

Abby Sofia, a secondary student, and John Diego, a 4th grader, make decisions at home naturally and constantly. What about in school, though? How many opportunities do they get to struggle through content, hypothesizing alternatives and weighing the options?

Ask yourself: What kinds of **deciding tasks** do you assign, and for what purposes? Then, with these tasks in mind, ask yourself the **i5 questions**:

1. How else could the students and I search for *information*?
2. How else could we use visual *images* and nonlinguistic representations to add meaning?
3. How could I encourage students to *interact* with others, live or through social media, to obtain and provide feedback?
4. How could I teach the *inquiry* skill—decision making—to deepen knowledge?
5. How could I plan for the students to use the application to generate *innovative* insights and products related to the lesson goals?

The Procedure

How did you decide which car to buy the last time you were in the market for one? Was cost or color a factor in your decision? Did you have to share the decision with a partner or a spouse? Was it easy? Did you ever experience remorse for making a decision too quickly? *I wish I had chosen the other shirt, car, or entrée.* We have all had that experience, haven't we? Although there are times when deciding might be a matter of flipping a coin, mastering the thinking skill of decision making—that is, methodically considering each of several alternatives and choosing an option based on their values—enables us to come to more robust and justifiable conclusions and fewer regrettable ones. Figure 6.2 shows the steps.

FIGURE 6.2
How to Make a Decision

The objective: Select from among seemingly equal choices.

Steps in the Process	Simplified Language
1. Describe a situation and the decision you want to make.	1. Describe a decision you want to make.
2. List the different alternatives you want to consider.	2. List your choices.
3. State various criteria that are important to consider and assign an importance score (e.g., 1–4).	3. List the features that are important to you to make the choice.
4. Rate each alternative on a scale (e.g., 1–4) to show the extent to which each alternative meets each criterion.	4. Give a number of tokens or marks to each feature to show its value.
5. For each alternative, multiply the importance score and the rating and then add the products to indicate a score for each alternative.	5. For each choice, now place those tokens or marks to show its importance.
6. Determine which alternative has the highest score and use it as your choice or to determine how you will take action.	6. Identify the choice with the highest number of tokens or marks and tell how you will take action.

In schools, students are exposed to all kinds of decisions, from those made by characters in stories or people in history to those made by scientists and by artistic creators and performers. Students see the result of these decisions, but they are not as likely to learn the process behind them: how scientists came to the point of a discovery or how that artist chose to use one technique over others. Decision making is ubiquitous, and school is a great place to teach a rigorous approach that can lead to a more nuanced understanding of great ideas and products—and to their creation.

Note, in Figure 6.2, how we can teach students to extend a simple comparison matrix into a decision-making one by adding the valuing steps after they have identified the characteristics and the items. Assigning value to the characteristics provides a way to separate the alternatives, and the question of what constitutes value in various contexts can generate intriguing ideas and support vigorous discussion.

In the Classroom: Lesson Examples

The Value of National Symbols

In her kindergarten class, Beth Talley taught a unit focused on symbols of the United States: the Liberty Bell, the Statue of Liberty, a bald eagle, the White House, and the American flag. The unit involved listening to readings about each of these symbols, but Mrs. Talley also wanted to be sure her students attained a solid grasp of the concept of symbols of democracy, so she chose to explicitly teach decision making to have students think about and decide which symbol was the most important.

Mrs. Talley supplemented trade books about each of the symbols with online sources and videos of people visiting the White House or Statue of Liberty or of an eagle soaring over rivers and meadows (*information, images*). She taught her kindergarten students a note-taking procedure that was mostly drawing pictographs. As a culminating task, the students referred to the notes and completed a decision-making matrix (*inquiry*) to decide the importance of each symbol. Instead of multiplying calculated scores, the kindergartners used beans to weight their choices and then worked as a group (*interaction*) to order the symbols from most important to least important.

The i5 Reflection: Mrs. Talley loved teaching decision making as part of this lesson because it gave students the chance to express their own ideas rather than just follow hers. They were engaged by this more active role, and engaged by the addition of video and images to provide real-world context to what, in prior years, had been more of a listening experience. The i5 approach, Mrs. Talley said, allowed her to let student questions guide the discussion rather than prompting most of the discussion in her usual way.

Almost Astronauts

Middle school science teacher McKinzie Sanders strives to make sure that her students, young men and women, understand that science is a field open to them all. In the past, she collaborated with an English teacher on an interdisciplinary task in which students wrote about possible career choices. This year, after reading online about the Mercury Thirteen, a group of women who trained as astronauts in 1959, at the same time as the original astronauts in the Mercury Seven, Ms. Sanders chose to explicitly teach students how to make career choices in science. (She'd seen the movie *The Right Stuff* and read the book it was based on, but it took the internet to teach her that there were at least 13 more people who had the right stuff to be an astronaut!)

To begin, Ms. Sanders led students first to the Mercury Thirteen website (www.mercury13.com), then to various other sites featuring vastly different careers that people chose to pursue in science, including ones about Carlos Juan Finlay, the Cuban scientist who found the link between mosquitoes and yellow fever in the 1800s; Charles Henry Turner, the first African American to earn a PhD from the University of Chicago (in 1907), who determined that insects can hear; and Dr. Virginia Apgar, who created the Apgar assessment tool to determine the well-being of newborns (*information* and *images)*. There were so many great examples that interested students—because of the discoveries these science professionals made, but also because of who these individuals were: names and faces typically overlooked in traditional history and science textbooks. Now, they were easily accessible with an online search.

Guided by the i5 approach, Ms. Sanders presented her students with the task of deciding on a personal career pathway in science (*inquiry*). She modeled using a decision-making matrix, and then students chose four career choices and worked in teams to gather information and share online resources. The two-day lesson ended with an electronic gallery walk where students shared their choices, along with brief explanations (*interaction*). This teacher's biggest surprise was how much sharing students were doing, and how excited they were about their findings and decisions; it was hard to stop the interaction even when the bell rang. They went on to collaborate on a class article for the school newspaper that shared their goals for the future, with specific examples of their choices for careers in science.

The i5 Reflection: Given online access to so many biographies, lists of famous scientists, and even explanations about careers, the lesson was very successful. Ms. Sanders commented on how a decision task "forces" students to gather information to secure both the alternatives as well as the criteria, and she confessed that without the i5 impetus to focus on a thinking skill, she simply would have had her students find one scientist to research and affirm their intention to make a similar career choice. The thinking skill and infinite access to the information that the digital devices provided elevated the opportunities and the discussions. It helped students generate their own career choices more realistically and made the task more personal and engaging.

Thinking in University

"Preparing preservice teachers begins with allowing them to be master learners themselves," says Adria Trombley. Mrs. Trombley teaches at a university with both undergraduate and graduate students. She makes sure that the students in her classes experience the GANAG lesson planning structure firsthand and takes the opportunity to teach the i5 approach as well.

During a recent break between semesters, Mrs. Trombley told Susan about a text for an upcoming graduate class that presented two opposing positions for issues facing public schools. A typical assignment would be read both positions, form your own opinion, and write about it in an essay. Realizing the content lent itself well to the application of a thinking skill, she decided to use decision making, knowing it would also help students read the material more critically. After learning more about incorporating information, images, and interaction with the inquiry skill, the students began to use decision making.

Prior to class, the students read a chapter that addressed religion and public schools. Mrs. Trombley taught the steps to create a decision-making matrix (inquiry) and explained how she went online to learn more about the First Amendment, the Supreme Court decisions mentioned in the text, and the justices who made the rulings (*information, images*). The students, some physically present and some connected online, discussed the values they assigned to each criterion (*interaction*). Once the matrices were completed, Mrs. Trombley posed a question: "How did using the inquiry skill affect your decision?" One student said it made her think about every option and every possibility; another explained that it gave her a basis to analyze how she came to her point of view and inspired her to do more research to see if she stayed with that decision. "I thought it was helpful, because I am very indecisive," commented another.

The assignment for the following week was to choose another chapter, read and research (*information, images*), complete a decision matrix (*inquiry*), create a presentation explaining his or her opinion, post it online, and then read and comment on two other students' posts (*interaction*). After completing the initial assignment, students were asked to create a brief position paper explaining how their position would affect their future classrooms (*innovation*).

The i5 Reflection: Mrs. Trombley worked in K–12 schools for a long time. She explained that bringing the lesson schema and the i5 to her university class increased the level of engagement of the students. They read and researched with purpose and considered positions they might not have considered without the aid of the thinking skill. Access to additional information and images online deepened their understanding of the text and added nuance to their opinions, all leading to them taking more confident positions on the topic at hand. Many of these students work in schools and went on to share how they could address the topic in their own districts.

Testing Hypotheses

Mark Twain had his head examined. The humorist, who knew his way around a hoax, was skeptical of phrenology, a pseudoscience popularized during the Victorian era, which held that the bumps and crevices on someone's skull could provide insight into that person's character. Rather than creating an argument against phrenology, Twain decided to test the science for himself.

As the story goes, Twain paid a visit to one of the Fowler brothers, both famous phrenologists, but he did not reveal his identity. During the session, the examiner told Twain that he had a bump on his skull indicating a person of enormous courage, but also a crevice characteristic of a cautious nature. The phrenologist concluded that, unfortunately, the cautious side overshadowed the courage, so Twain was best suited to a simple and ordinary life with a total absence of humor. Twain returned two months later, this time announcing himself as the famous comic author. Remarkably, this exam revealed no crevice of caution, and the courage bump had grown to proportions that indicated a sense of humor the size of Mount Everest!

This story appears in a book called *Brainwashed* (Satel & Lilienfield, 2013), which focuses the reader on the dangers of neuromania, or the tendency to oversell the power of neuroscientific investigation and use it as a tool to market all kinds of products and services. Although we are learning amazing truths about how the mind and brain work, much of what marketers claim to be backed by neuroscience is loosely connected at best.

Teaching students to generate and test hypotheses is a valuable lesson for students to apply to many situations, including science classrooms.

Ask yourself: What kinds of **hypothesis-testing tasks** do you assign, and for what purposes? Then, with these tasks in mind, ask yourself the **i5 questions**:

1. How else could the students and I search for *information?*
2. How else could we use visual *images* and nonlinguistic representations to add meaning?
3. How could I encourage students to *interact* with others, live or through social media, to obtain and provide feedback?
4. How could I teach the *inquiry* skill—hypothesis testing—to deepen knowledge?
5. How could I plan for the students to use the application to generate *innovative* insights and products related to the lesson goals?

The Procedure

Testing hypotheses is different from the other Taking Action processes because it involves creating an experiment or an instrument to gather data that will support a sound conclusion. Although it's habit to think of testing hypotheses as work confined to science experiments, testing is easily done in the humanities through surveys or focus groups. In the technical and arts areas, market testing is a key aspect of commercial products.

Many students' experience with testing hypotheses in schools involves learning to follow the prompts in a lab situation or to follow the directions on how to survey a population. A better approach focuses on having students internalize the steps for testing hypotheses so that it becomes a go-to skill—useful for them the way it was for Mark Twain. Figure 6.3 shows the steps.

FIGURE 6.3
How to Test Hypotheses

The objective: Observe, experiment, and explain.

Steps in the Process	Simplified Language
1. Observe an event or situation.	1. Observe an event or situation.
2. Explain what you observe and might infer.	2. Explain what you see or understand to be happening.
3. Make a prediction or state a hypothesis.	3. Predict something that can be tested.
4. Create a test or survey to test your prediction.	4. Set up a test or survey.
5. Collect data and organize the results.	5. Collect data and organize the results.
6. Draw a conclusion and use the findings to describe how to take action.	6. Use what you learned to take action.

In the Classroom: Lesson Examples

Lunar Landing

For years, a team of 3rd grade teachers taught a science lesson in which students used marshmallows to design a mock-up of a shock-absorbing system that would allow two astronauts to land safely on the Moon. The students enjoyed the hands-on task, but the teachers wondered how many of them actually grasped the scientific principle at work.

When working with these teachers, Susan suggested that they try to ask themselves the i5 questions, beginning with the first: Would adding *information* (from online sources) improve the learning outcome? Their subsequent information search turned up *Moonshot,* a fascinating book in which author Brian Floca (2009) provides detailed illustrations and diagrams on the stages of a launch, lunar insertion, and liftoff, including timelines of the events.

Next, the teachers focused on the second of the i5 questions—the one focused on *images* and *interaction.* This led them to find and guide students to use an interactive website designed for testing different ideas for lunar landing crafts. It was an ideal venue for students to apply the *inquiry* skill of generating and testing hypotheses.

Combining curricular content information about potential and kinetic energy with the detailed Apollo 11 information in *Moonshot,* students followed the steps for predicting and testing a lunar module prototype. Then, using cardboard, a plastic cup, index cards, regular marshmallows, miniature marshmallows, and rubber bands, the students went on to design their own model of a shock-absorbing lunar lander. They tested their prototypes and shared their findings. They made videos of the landers as they dropped them from different heights. If their model failed, they used what they had learned about potential and kinetic energy to change the lander and finalize their product.

The i5 Reflection: Learning new information about the first lunar landing was critical for students to better understand how to respond to the task. Using class iPads to record the landings provided opportunities to "see" the effects of potential and kinetic energy, increasing understanding of the concepts. The interactive website allowed students to engage with information individually, meaning they could explore the content that was most relevant to them and work at their own pace. Finally, teaching students the steps of creating a test or experiment increased the effectiveness of their engineering designs.

Functions in Mathematics

At a certain point in most lessons, at least one of Patrick Villarreal's 8th grade math students would pose the age-old question: "When will we ever *use* this?" Sometimes, the answer was easy to give, as in lessons where the math could be used to compare products or make decisions when measuring. When Mr. Villarreal was teaching functions, however, explaining the application was a little more challenging.

He decided to begin by looking for a relatable, real-life example, and landed on the county fair and rodeo—a favorite event in the community. At his prompting, the students wrote down the number of days they attended the recent fair, how many rides they went on, and how much food they ate. "You had the fun," Mr. Villarreal told them, "but someone had to do the math to make sure everything went smoothly." He then announced that everyone in the class had just been "elected" to the fair's Board of Directors, and their charge was increase the fair's revenue by either raising the entry fee or raising the price of the rides. Which tactic did they think would be more profitable? They needed to set up an experiment to test the different options before coming to a final new set of prices.

At this point, Mr. Villarreal posted the steps of testing a hypothesis (*inquiry*) and guided the class's consideration of the function $y = mx + b$ as a system, defining the parts like so:

y = the total cost of going to the fair
b = the entrance fee (currently $5.00)
m = the price per ride (currently $1.50)
x = the number of rides sold

Students set up the function as $y = 1.50x + 5.00$ and graphed the function, using both online graphing software and their handheld calculators. Next, Mr. Villarreal split the class into four groups and assigned each group a change to make to either the slope (m) or the y-intercept (b) of the function:

- Group 1: Change the slope (m) to 3.50 and keep the y-intercept (b) at 5.00.
- Group 2: Change the slope (m) to 0 and keep the y-intercept (b) at 5.00.
- Group 3: Change the y-intercept (b) to 3.00 and keep the slope (m) at 1.50.
- Group 4: Change the y-intercept (b) to 0.

Students then used calculators to graph the new functions and made note of what happened: how the function changed from the original. From that point, the students could consider other factors that might be changed (e.g., fees for parking, renting strollers or wheelchairs, guides). They went online to research what different amusement parks and events charged for these services (*information* and *images*), and they used functions to test different pricing structures and compared the revenue generated.

The i5 Reflection: Mr. Villarreal's i5 epiphany was that giving the students a familiar scenario would motivate them to want to generate answers. Teaching the idea of hypothesis in math made sense in the context of a problem that was relevant to the students' lives. It allowed students to veer away from getting "right answers" and toward seeing how organizations need to use math as the test for different options. Given the opportunity to see the dynamic aspect of mathematics, students were motivated to see other formulas in action.

Creating

Chip and Dan Heath focus on creativity in their book, *Made to Stick* (2007). They write about different success stories and then offer six principles, captured in the acronym SUCCESs, to ensure the generation of good ideas—ideas that are "sticky," meaning that they work, and work in different areas of human behavior.

The elements of the Heaths' SUCCESs approach are to make the idea **S**imple (get to the core), **U**nexpected (grab attention using both surprise and mystery), **C**oncrete (make it believable and aggreeable), and **E**motional (make a connection people will care about) and to convey the idea through **S**tories (choose an anecdote that will get people to take action).

Southwest Airlines, according to the SUCCESs story, did not just *decide* to become THE low-fare airline; they revised policies, procedures, and habits to be able to do so. The company set a clear goal, then made the necessary effort to revise how an airline operates so that it could offer that innovation.

Creating is the process we use to improve upon a situation or fill in a need. Unlike solving a problem, where the task is or can be defined by the obstacles, and unlike decision making, where the choice hangs in the balance, when creating, the student sets the standards and criteria. Creating is the process of making something new because you can. Knowing how and when to seek feedback from others is usually a positive aspect of creating; it can confirm or redirect the process.

Ask yourself: What kinds of **creation tasks** do you assign, and for what purposes? Then, with these tasks in mind, ask yourself the **i5 questions**:

1. How else could the students and I search for *information?*
2. How else could we use visual *images* and nonlinguistic representations to add meaning?
3. How could I encourage students to *interact* with others, live or through social media, to obtain and provide feedback?
4. How could I teach the *inquiry* skill—creating—to deepen knowledge?
5. How could I plan for the students to use the application to generate *innovative* insights and products related to the lesson goals?

The Procedure

It is fitting that this thinking skill wraps up the set of Taking Action strategies, because it defines self-regulation. The core of creating is observing that a situation could be bettered by generating an excellent new idea, product, or process. Each of the previous thinking skill processes concludes with its application to extend a collection of information, images, and interactive experiences into an innovation. Creating starts at this moment of innovation—when we need an idea, and we need it now—and proceeds through a process of deciding the outcome sought, making an attempt, gathering feedback, making revisions, and sharing the finished work.

Figure 6.4 shows the steps to teach the inquiry skill of creating.

FIGURE 6.4
How to Create

The objective: Design products or processes to meet standards and serve specific ends.

Steps in the Process	Simplified Language
1. Describe a need to meet or a desired end.	1. Think of something that needs to exist or be better.
2. Determine a set of standards for success.	2. Explain what it should look like or be like.
3. Design a prototype or a draft.	3. Make a model.
4. Seek feedback to improve on the idea or product.	4. Listen to what others have to say about how to make it better.
5. Edit or revise until the need appears to be met.	5. Make it better.
6. Take action to produce, publish, or share the innovation.	6. Produce, publish, or share it.

For teachers, makerspaces and project- or problem-based learning should come to mind. There are many schools today that provide facilities and class time for "creating" to encourage high levels of both discovery and independent work. However, using PBL in isolation may not be the most effective way to increase student achievement, according to John Hattie (2009). It falls in the very low effect size range of $d = 0.15$. Hattie reports much higher effect sizes for teaching problem solving ($d = 0.61$), creativity ($d = 0.67$), and metacognitive strategies ($d = 0.69$). However, PBL provides a perfect stage for engaging and motivating students *if* teachers can directly teach the inquiry steps for metacognition and creativity to advance student achievement. The i5 approach is a great companion for PBL, as it provides the steps for creating or a choice of other specific thinking skills students can use to increase learning.

The process of creating has two pivot points that mark the shift to higher learning: determining the standards for success (Step 2) and revising to make it better (Step 5). In class, just because an activity culminates in a product does not mean students are "creating." That process requires a plan, a set of standards to work toward, and the deliberate work of adjusting and revising.

In the Classroom: Lesson Examples
Hydration for Life

Kim Mason is an educational consultant from Kendrick Fincher Hydration for Life, a nonprofit dedicated to promoting proper hydration and avoiding heat-related illnesses. She approached Susan about incorporating proper hydration education into one grade level in Susan's school district. After a quick glance through the content standards, Kim and Susan decided 2nd grade would be an appropriate match. The foundation had compiled facts about hydration and incorporated them into songs and activity sheets, and Susan recognized that applying the i5 would enhance the learning experience.

After she explained the concept of the i5 to Kim, the pair decided to create a one week mini-unit that centered around 2nd graders creating personal hydration plans (*inquiry*). Susan suggested using TES Teach (www.tes.com/lessons) as a platform to house resources for the unit (*information, images*). She would share the link with the district's 2nd grade teachers, who could, in turn, share it with students or link resources from the platform to their Google Classrooms. Kim contributed by helping to create resources appropriate for 2nd graders. Here is the plan they mapped out:

> *Friday Prior to the Unit Start:* Ask students to log everything they drink over the weekend in a private journal.
>
> *Monday:* Introduce the concept of proper hydration, using a video and several infographics added to Google Classroom (*information, images*). Students use the application Padlet to enter a comment about what they learned in relation to the new information and their weekend journal entries (*interaction*).
>
> *Tuesday:* Explore the many health benefits of being properly hydrated. Review students' reflective comments on Padlet. Introduce the steps to the *create* inquiry skill (*inquiry*) and kick off the process by asking students to carry out Step 1 of the process: *Think about how they might create a new/better hydration plan for themselves.*
>
> *Wednesday:* Provide additional electronic resources about proper hydration (*information, images*) that the students can use to inform the creation of their personal hydration plan.
>
> *Thursday:* Incorporate a cooperative learning structure to allow students to share their hydration plans and receive feedback from peers (*interaction*).
>
> *Friday:* Students revise their plans, based on the feedback received, then publish them within Google Classroom.

The i5 Reflection: Applying the i5 to a real-world issue provides an opportunity for authentic application. Teaching the steps to create provides a vehicle for students to craft a useful plan for healthy living and lays a foundation that will be useful well beyond 2nd grade.

Getting Max Home

Scattered around the classroom, trios of kindergartners huddled over tubs of water, using a variety of tools to propel Styrofoam bowls ("boats") across mini-oceans. Academic vocabulary such as *push, pull,* and *force* floated through the air. A STEM challenge was in full swing—and it was the outcome of the work done by a team of teachers who had used the i5 approach to plan a lesson that would actively engage their students in using the forces *push* and *pull* to change the speed or direction of an object.

The original task had sprung from Maurice Sendak's Caldecott Award-winning *Where the Wild Things Are* (1963). The kindergartners were told they needed to get Max home. In addition to the bowl boats and water tub seas, they were provided with a teddy bear math manipulative to represent Max and a variety of construction materials, including straws, magnets, paperclips, and popsicle sticks. Working in teams, their charge was to move Max's boat without using their fingers. Although students always seemed to enjoy the challenge, the teachers confessed that the content focus tended to get lost, and it was difficult to assess students' performance of the desired standard. This was when Susan suggested that the teachers revise the challenge through the lens of the i5.

Using an online dashboard building application that accompanied their electronic science book, the teachers posted familiar videos, diagrams, and photographs to create a resource about *push* and *pull* that students could access from tablets (*information, images*) at any time during the challenge. The teachers assigned a role for each team member and located sentence starters to scaffold interactive conversations (*interaction)* and promote the use of academic vocabulary. They also adapted the steps of creating (*inquiry*) into "I can" statements that mirrored the Engineering Design Loop posters on the classroom walls and gave students specific learning targets.

The i5 Reflection: In this lesson's original form, students were simply presented with the challenge and released to start their work. Teachers assumed that students would draw on their new knowledge of forces and that the result would be a completed engineering design loop. However, the students did not seem to really connect the activity of moving the boat to what they were learning about forces *or* to the design loop.

By adopting the i5 approach and using the i5 questions to plan, the teachers created a framework that encouraged self-regulation in the process of creating. Students had access to information about the key concepts, a guide for collaborative conversations, and steps to direct the efforts to create a means of propelling Max home. The students set standards, created a plan, and then adjusted it based on feedback from the teacher and their peers.

Give Peace a Chance

Melissa Bonett, a secondary music teacher, realized that in the past, her students spent a lot of time on the procedural knowledge of music, but she wanted them to do more than just perform music—she wanted them to *know about it* too, and she wanted them to be able to use this knowledge to produce a unique product. One of the standards in her secondary music curriculum involved students being able to identify and connect the features and purposes of different kinds of music, both past and contemporary. Although Ms. Bonett knew her students were familiar with encountering expressions of protest and free speech via social media, she wondered how familiar they were with historical protest music. Focusing on this genre struck her as a great way to get students to explore music's role in communicating messages.

She kicked off the lesson by asking students to go online to view a chart that shows a Global Peace Index (www.visionofhumanity.org), which established a context for their consideration of the emergence of protest music (*information, images*). Which countries rank the highest in measures of peacefulness, and by which criteria? At the time of the lesson, Iceland and Portugal ranked as among the most peaceful nations, and Ms. Bonett showed students how to search for protest songs from those countries.

Following this initial activity, students accessed some of the websites Ms. Bonett had bookmarked for them. They read about and listened to songs linked to the abolition, temperance, child labor, and workers' rights movements. There was a lot to learn about protest music, why it was created, by whom, and during what time periods. The class assignment was to form groups, choose a topic, and compose and write lyrics for a modern protest song. Ms. Bonett provided standards for song length and topics, but students wrote and performed the songs themselves. As they conducted research about their topics and drafted their pieces, they shared them with classmates to obtain feedback to help them hone their messages (*interaction*).

The i5 Reflection: The i5 approach is perfect for teaching music, as online access to lyrics, audio recordings, and performance video enables students to cast a wide net when they're seeking information. Ms. Bonett noted that prior to i5, an assignment for this kind of content would probably have involved each student choosing a single artist, researching his or her life, and creating a presentation to share with the class. We have all seen and assigned these; they take a lot of time, and too often, the result is a big cut-and-paste job. With i5 guiding her lesson planning, however, she focused students on thinking and inquiry, setting up a collaborative task leading to creation.

Ms. Bonett admitted that because her students were engaged in performing arts and learning actively, they were simultaneously developing thinking skills. Appreciating the distinction between the procedural knowledge of practicing and the higher-order thinking application of declarative knowledge, characteristic of inquiry, led her to design a task that was both engaging and promoted deeper understanding.

Summary

Students take action all day long. In some cases, rash decisions, quick judgments, and hastily-produced work leads teachers to tell them that they should have "thought through" or "thought about" the task more.

What we mean by this is that students should have generated multiple solutions and not just one, built a decision-making matrix to weight choices based on valued criteria, set up a test to determine if something was true or viable, and exerted effort through relentless revision based on feedback.

The newest research on the prefrontal cortex suggests that students can learn the skills to generate great ideas and great innovations by researching the breadth of a subject online in addition to experience. The online environment can take them back hundreds of years to writings, images, and communications (through letters) about topics as different as the science behind the shape of eggs to the migration of peoples and their cultures. When students use the thinking skills of Taking Action, they have the opportunity to do more than just search for information; they have tools to use information to envision and create a better world.

7

Thinking About Teaching

Darius, a country boy, yearned to fly. In the story of his adventures, *Darius Green and His Flying-Machine,* told by John T. Trowbridge in a poem first published in1869, Darius the dreamer reasons as follows:

"Birds can fly
An' why can't I?
Must we give in,"
Says he with a grin,
"'T the bluebird an' phoebe
Are smarter'n we be?
Jest fold our hands an' see the swaller,
An' blackbird an' catbird beat us holler?"

At the turn of the 20th century, human flight was the new frontier. Some flew hot air balloons; others tried gliders to see if they could fly like the birds. It seemed that the better-built the wings on the machine, the more likely it might fly, so inventors designed bat wings, double-decker wings, and flexible wings. Supported by the Smithsonian Institution, Samuel P. Langley built "aerodromes" with better body designs and tandem wings and attempted the famous houseboat launch. Langley tried and tried. But it was the Wright brothers—the modest owners of a bicycle shop who focused not on the design of the wings but on the importance of stabilizing and steering the machine in flight—who succeeded first. David McCullough, author of *The Wright Brothers* (2015), writes that these bicycle mechanics understood something others didn't: one needed to apply the concept of equilibrium, the same principle of balance necessary to master riding a bicycle, to flying a plane. The Wright brothers' goal was to stay in the air longer, to travel further each time, and to perfect the art of controlling the flying machine. It's the Wright brothers who we remember.

By analogy, one can make a strong connection between the intense drive to master human aviation and the drive to bring about a technology revolution in our schools (see Figure 7.1).

FIGURE 7.1

Analogy: Flight and Technology Use in the Classroom

Topic of Enthusiasm	Flight	Technology in the Classroom
Goal	To develop a flying machine	To use digital devices in classrooms to improve learning
Early results	First attempts were not successful; the machines did not stay in the air	First attempts were not successful at producing gains in student learning
Key to solving the problem	Equilibrium (the Wright brothers)	The i5 approach and teaching thinking skills
Epiphany	It was necessary to practice controlling and steering the flight, and the machine design is the means to that end.	We need to teach critical and creative thinking—and technology is the means to that end.
Conclusion	The machine is not as important as the pilot who prepares for flight by factoring in weather and winds, steers, and applies lessons learned to the next flight.	The digital devices are not as critical as the teacher who prepares lessons and units, delivers instruction for thinking, and formatively assesses students to inform the next lessons.
Ultimate result	Longer flights, from takeoffs to flying to transportation	Improved learning, from recall to inference to innovation

As we progress through the 21st century, the idea of using technology in classrooms has created numerous enthusiasts—parents, school boards, teachers, and students alike. The passionate support for funds for 1:1 classrooms, paperless schools, and any use of technology eclipses most other instructional initiatives today. We have even seen technology become a key issue in state testing. Unfortunately, data does not confirm that using technology results in dramatically improved student performance.

The flight analogy suggests that there is a lesson to be learned from the history of flight, which is that the critical issue is not the machine or the technology but the underlying principle that must be understood and implemented to reach our goals. The i5 approach enables teachers to steer students toward using technology to help them become better thinkers and better innovators.

The Implementation Dip

Kenneth W. Eastwood, the superintendent of Middletown School District in New York, is aptly known as the "technology superintendent" because he has garnered remarkable fiduciary and human resources to support the low-income district with hardware, software, staff development, and partnerships. The district has moved ahead with a mission to incorporate blended learning, flipped classrooms, and makerspaces to encourage innovation in their curriculum. He is proud of their achievements; Middletown has a great international reputation.

Nevertheless, Dr. Eastwood listens to principals and teachers who have noticed that even with the newest software and devices, the district is experiencing the proverbial "implementation dip" in technology use. While the early adapters move ahead with the new initiatives, many staff members do not seem as enthusiastic. An implementation dip is a performance and confidence drop that occurs when adopting new practices. A leader may introduce an amazing idea, sell the idea to his or her constituents, and get out of the way for change to happen, but full-scale adoption does not happen. Many people in an organization seem to hold off or not try to adapt to the change while the organization itself moves ahead.

Dr. Eastwood said he was aware and even expected the dip, but he wanted to know why it would happen with teachers and technology. His concern, like ours, is that technology is a vital force and a critical ally in the effort to teach all students to become critical thinkers.

Dr. Eastwood's observations reminded Jane of Ted Sizer's fictitious teacher, Horace Smith, who resisted change. Horace's character was the iconic English teacher at Franklin High School in the book *Horace's Compromise* (1984). Sizer wrote the book just after the publication of the report *A Nation at Risk* (National Commission on Excellence in Education, 1983), which painted U.S. schools in an unfavorable light.

To find a way to encourage excellence in schooling, Sizer wrote about the fictional high school where the suggested reforms were largely related to calendar and contact hours, creating teacher teams for better communication, graduation standards, workplace skills, and mainstreaming students with disabilities. Reforms were introduced to "fix" schools, but the tacit understanding among Horace and the teachers and students was "Give a little, get along, compromise" (Sizer, 1984, p. 7). Horace was a good teacher. He had worked for a long time. And he intended to keep doing what he had always done before. Why change?

Horace epitomizes the implementation dip. Every teacher in one way or another has the potential to become Horace; teaching can become a habit, best accomplished expecting a normal curve of student performances. Although Horace admitted that he wanted better resources, more interested parents, fewer faculty meetings, and self-directed students, he enjoyed feeling self-employed, and he resisted anything new.

What would Horace do in a 1:1 classroom today? Technology initiatives have provided what Horace wanted. We have much better resources for teachers that allow for real-time communication with parents, better access to information through online materials so less need for meetings, opportunities for creating and curating lessons, online staff development, and chances to make real change in learning through personalization so students can self-regulate. So how is it that we would

still find "Horaces" in school buildings today? Why is there an implementation dip when it comes to using technology in the classroom?

The truth is that an initiative that encourages students to bring a
highly distracting item (a personal digital device) to class with them is
sure to bring out the Horace in us all. Maybe Horace sees technology as
another doomed-to-fail iteration of a flying machine? After all, he has
seen many such initiatives crash and burn. So, the implementation dip
may be a result of the way some teachers "give a little, get along, compromise" in today's schools. But that does not work for a superintendent like Dr. Eastwood.

Adult Learning Theory

Maybe the obstacle preventing teachers from getting on board with
technology and thinking skill instruction is not an actual dip but a natural process, as described in adult learning theory. Principal Ebonique
"Nicole" Holloman also observed early adapters and initial resistors, so
she attempted to update professional development (PD) opportunities
for her K–8 staff. Deeply interested in building a community of adult,
as well as student, learners, she read about Malcolm Knowles's work dis-
tinguishing andragogy (adult learning) from pedagogy (student learning) (Bates, 2009). Knowles writes about five characteristics of adult
learners, including that they tend to be self-directed, draw from years of
personal experience when approaching new learning, and prefer solving problems through personal motivation, not external factors. Instead
of following traditional practice, Ms. Holloman organized inclusive PD
onsite, personalizing the meetings for shorter sessions that met consis-
tently each month and in a blended learning format. But she still found
that some of the teachers were having difficulty with the pedagogical
initiative.

Staff development has changed dramatically from the 1980s to
today to meet the needs of adult learners. But trainings on working
with adults, peer coaching, and varying agendas providing differentiation for teachers sometimes still results in resistance from education

professionals. Even with substantial research and application of adult learning theories, Horace is in our schools today.

Digital Immigrants and Digital Natives

Perhaps Dr. Eastwood and Ms. Holloman should consider the often-cited dilemma of digital immigrants versus digital natives. Frank Korb, an art teacher who started his teaching career in 1990, might refer to himself as a digital immigrant. He was excited when he learned to send out his very first e-mail. But three months passed before he sent out a second e-mail, and that was only because he had to send it to reserve his spot for a staff development training on technology. His "immigration" from the privacy of his print world to the digital world of global communications has been a slow one. Mr. Korb was comfortable with his 20 years of teaching routines, which did not include electronic devices, and he did not mind being identified as a digital immigrant.

Courtney Bryant, by contrast, is a digital native who was born in 1990. She began to teach in the fall of 2013. Like her Generation Y peers, Mrs. Bryant texts instead of calls, reads news online, taps a GPS on her phone for directions, orders shoes from a website, pays for a coffee with an app, and would have no idea what to do with a cassette tape and player if she encountered them.

"I could not wait to bring all of my new ideas to the classroom," Mrs. Bryant gushed. Yet three months after starting her new job, she found herself following the familiar routines she had watched for so many years as a student. Despite her personal digital expertise, Mrs. Bryant taught very much like her own school teachers did, only using technology occasionally in her teaching practice. She was stuck in "pedagogical automaticity"—she had absorbed the pedagogical practices she had observed for two decades as a student when teachers did not have devices and likely were not explicitly teaching thinking.

Habits

James Stigler and James Hiebert, authors of *The Teaching Gap* (1999), identify teaching as a cultural activity, much like a family dinner. We participate in family dinners in an automatized and effortless fashion, not realizing that all the processes we take for granted were learned by observation. Similarly, teaching is learned through attending school for a long period of time, observing the behaviors of teachers, and learning routines of schooling. Courtney Bryant teaches like her teachers taught, because after so many years in a classroom, their approaches became, for her, what teaching was. Let's take a moment to consider that by grade 9, most children have spent nearly 10,000 hours observing teaching—enough time, some might say, to make them experts.

In his book *The Power of Habit: Why We Do What We Do in Life and Business*, Pulitzer Prize-winning journalist Charles Duhigg writes, "Habits, scientists say, emerge because the brain is constantly looking for ways to save effort," (2014, p. 17). No doubt we all agree that a teacher's day can be extremely busy, so it is no surprise that a teacher would try to find ways to save effort. Pedagogical automaticity *can* be positive and useful—if teachers are satisfied with student engagement, achievement, and social interactions. However, if some students are academically at risk, then a teacher may need to change aspects of his or her pedagogical automaticity to improve student performance. This can be difficult for the Horaces, who want to "give a little, get along, compromise" (Sizer, 1984, p. 7). Remember, they don't want to change what is working for them. Teachers must be attuned to the need to change their habits based on how well students perform on a day-to-day and week-by-week basis.

The Golden Rule of Habit Change

According to Duhigg (2014), the Golden Rule of Habit Change is "You can't extinguish a bad habit, you can only change it." A habit involves a cue, a routine, and a reward.

Duhigg continues:

> In the past decade, our understanding of the neurology and psy-
> chology of habits and the way patterns work within our lives, soci-
> eties, and organizations has expanded in ways we couldn't have
> imagined fifty years ago. We now know the science behind why hab-
> its emerge, how they change, and their mechanics. We know how
> to break them into parts and rebuild them to our specifications....
> Transforming a habit isn't necessarily easy or quick. It isn't always
> simple. But it is possible. And now we understand how. (p. 63)

The way to change a habit is to keep the old cue and deliver the old
reward, but insert a new routine in between. You swap one habit for
another. Almost any behavior can be transformed if the cue and reward
stay the same. Duhigg explains that habits "create neurological crav-
ings" (2014, p. 47); to overpower the habit, we must recognize which
craving is driving the behavior.

Duhigg extends the personal example to habits seen in organizations and in society in general. Perhaps a school district is interested
in changing teaching habits so that teachers use technology to improve
thinking. Teachers are cued to teach when the students come in the
room; the routine is a combination of presenting material and discussion followed by giving students a task to work on in class; and the
reward is that the content was successfully covered in the class period.
The reward for most teachers is to cover the material for that day.

Imagine that a teacher tries to change his or her routine to incorporate technology into the lesson. The students come in the room (cue),
and the teacher instates the altered routine. In this case, using technology leads to distraction, socialization, and other device-related issues,
and the teacher's reward of covering the material is not achieved. Clearly,
the teacher will become frustrated with using technology because the
lesson does not work as well as it used to. So, we get another Horace—
and see an implementation dip.

One problem is that many teachers see the reward as covering content in the allotted time frame. Instead, the reward should be clear

evidence that students learned because that teacher taught that lesson. This conundrum, invisible in plain sight, leads to the implementation dip. Horace does not want to use digital devices in class because it might change the routine and interfere with his reward of getting through the material he must teach.

This book is an argument for changing the cue, the routine, *and* the reward using the i5 approach. The new teaching habit we want to instill looks like this:

1. **Cue**—Students enter, and the teacher begins the lesson by providing the goal—or learning intention. With the GANAG schema and the i5, the goal is a *student goal* or what he and she can learn better by the end of class.

2. **Routine**—The teacher teaches the lesson, delivering the content. But he or she also teaches students to use digital devices to expand their knowledge base by accessing better *information*, *images*, and formative feedback through *interaction* to more deeply understand the topics; they use *inquiry* skills to deeply generate new ideas and *innovations*. Technology engenders personalization and real-time communication. The routine changes from the old habit of the teacher needing to cover the material during one class period to a routine that focuses on ensuring that students access enough material in class or learn what they can do to use devices outside of class time to be able to practice or think about the topic.

3. **Reward**—The i5 approach allows teachers to see and hear students' own assessment of how well they learned the content of the lesson. The reward now is personalized student learning.

To increase technology use, a teacher can use the Golden Rule to change his or her habit. The goal is no longer to cover the material in a class period, but to ensure that all students actively learn the content and achieve the lesson goal. Using the i5 approach is a way to incorporate both technology and explicit thinking-skills instruction into lesson planning and delivery; this can help teachers change the reward from expecting improved teaching to expecting improved learning. Horace would like that; he wanted his students to be self-directed, but his habits inadvertently stood in the way. The personalization aspect of technology improves the learning.

Take Flight

Sunday night found Frank Korb—a digital immigrant rather than a digital native—word-processing his goals for the week's lessons into each class's blog: one goal for Art Foundations about line and space; two goals for Painting about color and blending techniques; and one goal for the Advanced Art class that addressed cultural voice and critical viewing. Done. Click and save.

Satisfied, Mr. Korb went to bed. The next morning, when his students awoke and checked their e-mail, they had a message from the blog that showed the goals for the day. At the beginning of class, Mr. Korb again shared the goals on the interactive whiteboard so the students could add them to their interactive notebooks.

As the lesson progressed, Mr. Korb modeled some techniques live but recorded them so that students could review the demonstrations as needed later, on their digital devices. The recordings enabled them to compare their work or analyze perspectives. They could also use their internet access to investigate historical artistic techniques and decide which ones to use in their own projects. The end-of-class cleanup included students snapping an image of their works-in-progress to upload to the shared drive for viewing. The students also self-assessed their progress toward the goal for the day using an online spreadsheet shared with their teacher.

Mr. Korb told us that technology has changed his teaching, but not in the ways that most people might think. "Using technology has made my preparation, delivery, and communication with students more efficient," he said. "When people ask me if I have started to use technology in my visual arts classes, I have to pause to think about it. Technology use has become just that automatic to me, as if I had always taught using these tools."

Mr. Korb added this:

> I have changed a lot about my teaching, but mostly I've improved my ability to teach thinking skills and provide feedback to students because we use our devices. I'm teaching students to think and produce better products now that I teach thinking explicitly, and I'm able to curate materials that may become resources later—all because of using technology in my classroom. It sounds clichéd, but I feel like I have transformed my 20th century teaching to 21st century learning using the i5 framework. The i5 reminded me of the importance that the goal of teaching is learning. And that the goal for using technology is not to use the tool, but to think.

The i5 approach is a way forward for teachers who struggle to figure out how to adapt their lessons to incorporate classroom technology in a way that leads to deep and lasting learning. Step 1 is to look at your lesson planning schema. Does it directly address teaching thinking as well as teaching procedural knowledge? Step 2 is to analyze your own Golden Rule of Habit. Is your reward to cover the material, or to know how well all students are learning? If you decide to change your pedagogical automaticity, you might try the i5 approach. Step 3 is to consider the technology. Dr. Eastwood, the "technology superintendent," told us that he believes good pedagogy trumps technology. He continued:

> That being said, good pedagogy and smart technology integration are very powerful thrusters for personalizing education. With the continual increase in student ability levels of students within the typical classroom, success for ALL students will require personalizing education by ALL teachers for ALL students. Teaching to the center will only produce less and less successful students. Changing teaching to using the i5 is not easy; but then, neither was designing and implementing successful flight. Successful teaching or airplane construction is difficult... but look at the rewards!

Under the Lamp Post

At the beginning of the book, Jane described the story about searching for keys in the place where the light was better. There, she found the i5 approach to planning and delivering instruction to teach thinking by using technology.

Teaching is the science of probing, poking, bumbling, and bungling through all available resources to prepare and deliver lessons. Teaching is discovering ways, including technology-infused ones, to teach all children in school to probe, poke, bumble, and bungle through all available resources to learn deeply so they can be contributing individuals who generate new insights for their generation and those to come. *The i5 approach is exhilarating.*

Appendix:
Thinking Skills Processes

Compare: Describe how items are the same or different.
1. Identify the items to compare. (Comparing three or more items makes the comparison more ambiguous and, therefore, more complex.)
2. Identify features by which to associate the items.
3. State how the items are similar or different based on the features.
4. Summarize findings to generate new ideas or insights.

Simplified Language
1. Name the items to compare.
2. Tell some features about the items.
3. Say how the items are the same or different based on the features.
4. Tell what you know now (share a new idea) or could do with the information (create a new product).

Classify: Group items together based on shared traits.
1. Identify multiple items to sort.
2. Sort the items based on a single or multiple attributes.
3. Reorganize or regroup items.
4. Summarize findings to generate new ideas or products.

Simplified Language
1. Name items to classify.
2. Sort the items and say why they are in a group.
3. Say how items could go into different groups.
4. Tell what you know now (share a new idea) or could do with the information (create a new product).

Create Analogies: Identify a relationship or pattern between a known and an unknown situation.
1. Identify an event or topic that is difficult to understand.
2. Identify a familiar situation describing the steps or the parts in general terms.
3. Explain the new event or topic using the familiar situation to guide the narrative.
4. Summarize understandings and generate insights about the new event or topic.

Simplified Language
1. Tell about a topic that is hard to understand.
2. Explain a familiar story or experience in your own words.
3. Tell how each part of what you know works, so you can explain the new topic.
4. Tell what you know now (share a new idea) or could do with the information (create a new product).

————————————— Synthesis —————————————

Investigate: Explain the theme of a topic, including anything that is ambiguous or contradictory.
1. Identify a topic to study or research.
2. State the ambiguity or contradiction about the topic and gather information.
3. Clarify the ambiguous or contradictory issues to extract the theme and gather more information, if necessary.
4. Summarize understandings and generate insights about the topic.

Simplified Language
1. Describe something or something that happened.
2. Say the main idea about the topic, or what is unique or unusual about it.
3. Read and gather information to explain the confusion.
4. Tell what you know now (share a new idea) or could do with the information (create a new product).

Argue: Make a claim supported by evidence and examples.
1. Describe an event or issue.
2. Prepare and state a claim defending, refuting, or reflecting on the topic.
3. Provide detailed evidence and elaboration about the claim.
4. Offer a counterclaim with support.
5. Summarize and use the findings to generate a new insight about the event or issue.

Simplified Language
1. Tell about a situation.
2. State your opinion about the situation.
3. Explain your opinion with examples.
4. State an opposite opinion about the situation.
5. Tell what you know now or how to make the situation better.

—————————————— Analysis ——————————————

Analyze Perspectives: Consider multiple takes on an issue.
1. Describe an event or issue.
2. State a viewpoint that is expressed, supported by logic and evidence.
3. Explain other viewpoints expressed, referencing supporting logic and evidence.
4. Explain the strengths, weaknesses, and unique features of the different viewpoints.
5. Summarize and use the findings to generate a new insight about the event or issue.

Simplified Language
1. Describe a situation.
2. Tell how one person sees it.
3. Tell how a different person sees it.
4. Give your opinion about the differences.
5. Explain what you know now or how to make it better.

Analyze Systems: Know how the parts of a system impact the whole.
1. Identify an object, event, or thing as a system.
2. Describe its parts and how they function.
3. Change a part or function and explain how it affects the whole.
4. Change another part and explain the results. (This step can be repeated multiple times.)
5. Summarize and use the findings to generate deeper understanding or an improvement to the system.

Simplified Language
1. Name something you will think about as a system.
2. Tell how the parts of it work.
3. Change one part and tell how the whole thing works now.
4. Do it again with a different part.
5. Explain what you know now about the thing or how to make it better.

Analyze Reasoning for Error: Recognize errors in thinking.
1. Describe an event, situation, or argument that is presented to you.
2. Identify the tactics (fallacies) used to manipulate the truth.
3. Explain possible misunderstandings based on the error in reasoning.
4. Summarize and use findings to generate a new idea or product.

Simplified Language
1. Tell about a situation or opinion.
2. Say what the presenter is trying to get you to believe.
3. Explain what might not be true.
4. Explain what you believe to be true.

---------- **Taking Action** ----------

Solve: Navigate obstacles to find a good solution to a problem.
1. Describe a situation that involves a goal.
2. Explain a barrier or barriers that prevent accomplishing the goal.
3. Identify multiple solutions to meet the goal.
4. Try a solution to overcome the barrier.
5. Repeat with other solutions.
6. Explain which solution you will use and how you will take action.

Simplified Language
1. Identify a goal.
2. Explain something that gets in the way of reaching the goal.
3. Identify a few ways to solve the problem.
4. Try one of the ways to see how it works.
5. Try another way.
6. Use what you learned to take action.

Decide: Select from among seemingly equal choices.
1. Describe a situation and the decision you want to make.
2. List the different alternatives you want to consider.
3. State various criteria that are important to consider and assign an importance score (e.g., 1–4).
4. Rate each alternative on a scale (e.g., 1–4) to show the extent to which each alternative meets each criterion.
5. For each alternative, multiply the importance score and the rating and then add the products to indicate a score for each alternative.
6. Determine which alternative has the highest score and use it as your choice or to determine how you will take action.

Simplified Language
1. Describe a decision you want to make.
2. List your choices.
3. List the features that are important to you to make the choice.
4. Give a number of tokens or marks to each feature to show its value.
5. For each choice, now place those tokens or marks to show importance.

6. Identify the choice with the highest number of tokens or marks and tell how you will take action.

Test: Observe, experiment, and explain.
1. Observe an event or situation.
2. Explain what you observe and might infer.
3. Make a prediction or state a hypothesis.
4. Create a test or survey to test your prediction.
5. Collect data and organize the results.
6. Draw a conclusion and use findings to describe how to take action.

Simplified Language
1. Observe an event or situation.
2. Explain what you see or understand to be happening.
3. Predict something that can be tested.
4. Set up a test or survey.
5. Collect data and organize the results.
6. Use what you learned to take action.

Create: Design products or processes to meet standards and serve specific ends.
1. Describe a need to meet or a desired end.
2. Determine a set of standards for success.
3. Design a prototype or a draft.
4. Seek feedback to improve on the idea or product.
5. Edit or revise until the need appears to be met.
6. Take action to produce, publish, or share the innovation.

Simplified Language
1. Think of something that needs to exist or be better.
2. Explain what it should look like or be like.
3. Make a model.
4. Listen to what others have to say about how to make it better.
5. Make it better.
6. Produce, publish, or share it.

Acknowledgments

We want to thank so many teachers and educators—friends of ours. Thanks to all the teachers and administrators who contributed to the book, including Veronica Armstrong, Donna Martin, Belinda Parini, Lauren Eide, Becky Efurd, Alina Mejia, Frank Korb, Jennifer Rivas, Natalie DeBrincat, Rusty Bishop, Megan McDermid, Julie Finney, Matt Keiser, Trisha Grayson, Deborah Goff, Lauren McCalman, George Santos, Robert Hammer, Steve Fougere, Beth Talley, McKinzie Sanders, Patrick Villarreal, Kim Mason, Melissa Bonett, Ken W. Eastwood, Ebonique "Nikki" Holloman, Diane Quirk, Jenny Felts, Anna Johnson, Sharla Osbourn, Leah Padilla, Marie Jeffrey, Courtney Bryant, Adria Trombley, and Virginia Abernathy.

Susan's colleagues at Rogers School District in Arkansas have been amazing in sharing their lessons, classrooms, and time.

To our colleagues Ian Mulligan, Ron Wence, and Gary Nunnally: we want to say thanks again for always listening and asking the right questions. We truly appreciate all our discussions about improving student learning.

Katie Martin, editor of all of Jane's books with ASCD, contributes in ways that readers could not realize. Katie and Genny Ostertag, director of Content Acquisitions, are as enthusiastic about providing the best read for teachers as we are, so thanks so much! Again!

References

Anderson, L. W., & Krathwohl, D. R. (Eds.) (2001). *A taxonomy for learning, teaching, and assessing: A revision of Bloom's taxonomy of educational objectives.* New York: Longman.

Bainbridge, D. (2008). *Beyond the zonules of zinn: A fantastic journey through your brain.* Cambridge, MA: Harvard University Press.

Bates, C. (2009). *Malcolm Knowles (1913–1997).* Retrieved from: http://web.utk.edu/~start6/knowles/malcolm_knowles.html

Bloom, B. (Ed.). (1956). *Taxonomy of educational objectives: The classification of educational goals, by a committee of college and university examiners.* New York: Longmans, Green.

BSCS. (2016). BSCS 5E Instructional Model. Retrieved from https://bscs.org/bscs-5e-instructional-model

Calkins, L. M. (1986). *The art of teaching writing.* Portsmouth, NH: Heinemann.

Cameron, A. (1981). *The stories Julian tells.* New York: Random House.

Campbell, G. (2012). *Are you sure? The unconscious origins of certainty.* N.p.: JENTS.

Carr, N. (2011). *The shallows: What the internet is doing to our brains.* New York: W. W. Norton.

Corkin, S. (2013). *Permanent present tense: The unforgettable life of the amnesic patient, H. M.* New York: Basic Books.

Costa, A. (Ed.) (1985). *Developing minds: A resource book for teaching thinking.* Alexandria: ASCD.

Covey, S. (2011). *The 3rd alternative: Solving life's most difficult problems.* New York: Free Press.

Cox, J. (2015, December). Benefits of technology in the classroom. Retrieved from http://www.teachhub.com/benefits-technology-classroom

de Bono, E. (1986). *CoRT Thinking*. Elmsford, NY: Pergamom Press Offices.

Doidge, N. (2007). *The brain that changes itself: Stories of personal triumph from the frontiers of brain science*. New York: Viking.

Duhigg, C. (2014). *The power of habit: Why we do what we do in life and business*. New York: Random House Trade Paperbacks.

Duke, N. K., & Pearson, P. (2002). Effective practices for developing reading comprehension. In Alan E. Farstrup & S. Jay Samuels (Eds.), *What research has to say about reading instruction* (3rd ed., pp. 205–242). Newark, DE: International Reading Association, Inc.

Feuerstein, R. (1980). *Instrumental enrichment: An intervention program for cognitive modifiability*. Baltimore: University Park Press.

Firestein, S. (2012). *Ignorance: How it drives science*. New York: Oxford University Press.

Fleischman, P. (1993). *Bull Run*. New York: HarperCollins.

Floca, B. (2009). *Moonshot: The flight of Apollo 11*. New York: Atheneum Books for Young Readers.

Goldberg, E. (2009). *The new executive brain: Frontal lobes in a complex world*. New York: Oxford University Press.

Grasty, T. (2012, April 3). The difference between "invention" and "innovation" [blog post]. Retrieved from http://www.huffingtonpost.com/tom-grasty/technological-inventions-and-innovation_b_1397085.html

Graves, D. H. (1983). *Writing: Teachers and children at work*. Exeter, NH: Heinemann Educational Books.

Hammond's Candies. (2011, May 10). The Oops Room [blog post]. *Hammond's Candies Blog and Recent Candy News*. Retrieved from https://hammond-scandies.worldsecuresystems.com/_blog/Hammonds_Candy_Blog/post/The_Oops_Room/

Hattie, J. (2009). *Visible learning: A synthesis of over 800 meta-analyses relating to achievement*. New York: Routledge.

Heath, C., & Heath, D. (2007). *Made to stick: Why some ideas survive and others die*. New York: Random House.

Hunter, M. (1994). *Mastery teaching: Increasing instructional effectiveness in elementary and secondary schools, colleges, and universities*. Thousand Oaks, CA: Corwin.

Hurson, T. (2008). *Think better (your company's future depends on it—and so does yours): An innovator's guide to productive thinking*. New York: McGraw-Hill.

Independence Hall Association. (n.d.). The invention of the teenager [web page]. *USHistory.org*. Retrieved from http://www.ushistory.org/us/46c.asp

International Society for Technology Education (ISTE). (2016). ISTE standards. Retrieved from http://www.iste.org/standards/standards/iste-standards

Karplus, R., & Thier, H. D. (1967). *A new look at elementary school science*. Chicago: Rand McNally & Company.

Kean, S. (2010). *The disappearing spoon: and other tales of madness, love, and the history of the world from the periodic table of the elements.* New York: Little, Brown, and Company.

Lear, E. (1846). There was an old man with a beard. *A book of nonsense.* Retrieved from http://www.nonsenselit.org/Lear/Bon/bon010.html

Marzano, R. J., Pickering, D. J., Arredondo, D., Blackburn, G., Brandt, R., Moffett, C., Paynter, D., Pollock, J., & Whisler, J. S. (1997). *Dimensions of learning teacher's manual* (2nd ed.). Alexandria, VA: ASCD.

Marzano, R. J., Pickering, D. J., & Pollock, J. E. (2001). *Classroom instruction that works: Research-based strategies for increasing student achievement.* Alexandria, VA: ASCD.

McCullough, D. (2015). *The Wright brothers.* New York: Simon & Schuster.

Michelangelo. (1508–1512). *Creation of Adam* [Fresco]. Sistine Chapel, Vatican City State.

Mueller, P. A., & Oppenheimer, D. M. (2014, April 23). The pen is mightier than the keyboard: Advantages of longhand over laptop note taking. *Psychological Science Online.* Retrieved from https://sites.udel.edu/victorp/files/2010/11/Psychological-Science-2014-Mueller-0956797614524581-1u0h0yu.pdf

National Association of Elementary School Principals. (2013, May). *How do parents feel about technology in the classroom?* Retrieved from http://www.naesp.org/communicator-may-2013/how-do-parents-feel-about-technology-classroom

National Commission on Excellence in Education. (1983). *A nation at risk: The imperative for educational reform: A report to the nation and the secretary of education, United States Department of Education.* Washington, DC: The Commission.

Panksepp, J., & Biven, L. (2012). *The archaeology of mind: Neuroevolutionary origins of human emotions* (Norton Series on Interpersonal Neurobiology) [Kindle Dx version]. Retrieved from Amazon.com.

Partnership for 21st Century Learning. (n.d.). Framework for 21st century learning. Retrieved from http://www.p21.org/about-us/p21-framework

Paul, R., & Elder, L. (2014). *Critical thinking: Tools for taking charge of your professional and personal life* (4th ed.). Indianapolis, IN: FT Press. First edition published 1985.

Pearson, P. D., & Gallagher, G. (1983, July). The instruction on reading comprehension. *Contemporary Educational Psychology, 8(17)*, 317–344.

Pollack, J. (2015). *Shortcut: How analogies reveal connections, spark innovation, and sell our greatest ideas.* New York: Gotham Books.

Pollock, J. E. (2007). *Improving student learning one teacher at a time.* Alexandria, VA: ASCD.

Ramachandran, V. S. (2011). *The tell-tale brain: A neuroscientist's quest for what makes us human.* New York: W. W. Norton.

Ratey, J. J. (2008). *Spark: The revolutionary new science of exercise and the brain.* New York: Little, Brown.

Satel, S., & Lilienfeld, S. O. (2013). *Brainwashed: The seductive appeal of mindless neuroscience.* New York: Basic Books.

Sendak, M. (1963). *Where the wild things are.* New York: Harper & Row

Shannon, D. (1998). *No, David!* New York: Blue Sky Press.

Shannon, D. (1999). *David goes to school.* New York: Blue Sky Press.

Shannon, D. (2002). *David gets in trouble.* New York: Blue Sky Press.

Simanek, D. (2014). Horse's teeth. Retrieved from https://www.lhup.edu/~dsimanek/horse.htm

Sizer, T. R. (1984). *Horace's compromise: The dilemma of the American high school: The first report from a study of high schools, co-sponsored by the National Association of Secondary School Principals and the Commission on Educational Issues of the National Association of Independent Schools.* Boston: Houghton Mifflin.

Stigler, J. W., & Hiebert, J. (1999). *The teaching gap: Best ideas from the world's teachers for improving education in the classroom.* New York: Free Press.

Trilling, B., & Fadel, C. (2009). *21st century skills: Learning for life in our times.* San Francisco: Jossey-Bass.

Trowbridge, J. T. (1869). *Darius Green and his flying-machine.* Boston: Houghton Mifflin. Retrieved from https://books.google.com/books/about/Darius_Green_and_His_Flying_machine.html?id=YuJoVVXZLTIC

Visual Teaching Alliance. (n.d.). Why visual teaching. Retrieved from http://visual-teachingalliance.com/

Williams, K. L., & Mohammed, K. (2007). *Four feet, two sandals.* Grand Rapids, MI: Eerdmans Books for Young Readers.

Willingham, D. T. (2007, Summer). Critical thinking: Why is it so hard to teach? *American Educator,* 8–18.

Willingham, D. T. (2009). *Why don't students like school? A cognitive scientist answers questions about how the mind works and what it means for the classroom.* San Francisco: Jossey-Bass.

Index

The letter *f* following a page number denotes a figure. GANAG steps are show in all CAPS.

About the Authors

 Jane E. Pollock, coauthor of the ASCD best-seller *Classroom Instruction That Works* (2001), collaborates worldwide with teachers, instructional coaches, and principals on curriculum, instruction, assessment, and supervision. Her work results in improved student achievement at the classroom and school levels.

A former classroom and English language teacher, Pollock worked as a district administrator and senior researcher for McREL Research Laboratory. She is president of Learning Horizon, Inc.

Pollock is the author of *Improving Student Learning One Teacher at a Time* (2007) and *Feedback: The Hinge that Joins Teaching and Learning* (2011). In addition to *Classroom Instruction That Works*, she coauthored *Dimensions of Learning Teacher and Training Manuals* (1996), *Assessment, Grading, and Record Keeping* (1999), *Improving Student Learning One Principal at a Time* (2009) and *Minding the Achievement Gap One Classroom at a Time* (2012).

A native of Caracas, Venezuela, Pollock earned degrees at the University of Colorado and Duke University. She can be reached at jpollock @learninghorizon.net.

 **Susan M. Hensley** is a practicing educator who contributed to Jane E. Pollock's *Minding the Achievement Gap One Classroom at a Time*, explaining the ways that she helps teachers motivate students to learn better by using research-based strategies.

Hensley taught at the elementary level, served as a literacy facilitator and curriculum specialist, and now works as a K–8 executive director of curriculum and instruction for Rogers Public Schools in Rogers, Arkansas.

She earned degrees at the University of Arkansas in Fayetteville and John Brown University, has an ESOL endorsement, and is a Northwest Arkansas National Writing Project Teacher Consultant. She can be reached at smariehensley@gmail.com.

Related ASCD Resources

At the time of publication, the following resources were available (ASCD stock numbers in parentheses):

PD Online® Courses

Dimensions of Learning: The Basics, 2nd Edition (#PD11OC128)

Technology in Schools: A Balanced Perspective, 2nd Edition (#PD11OC109M)

Print Products

Cultivating Curiosity in K–12 Classrooms: How to Promote and Sustain Deep Learning by Wendy L. Ostroff (#116001)

How to Assess Higher-Order Thinking Skills in Your Classroom by Susan M. Brookhart (#109111)

Improving Student Learning One Teacher at a Time (EBOOK) by Jane E. Pollock (#107005)

Sparking Student Creativity: Practical Ways to Promote Innovative Thinking and Problem Solving by Patti Drapeau (#115007)

Tasks Before Apps: Designing Rigorous Learning in a Tech-Rich Classroom by Monica Burns (#118019)

Teaching the 4 Cs with Technology: How do I use 21st century tools to teach 21st century skills? (ASCD Arias) by Stephanie Smith Budhai and Laura McLaughlin Taddei (#116038)

Using Technology with Classroom Instruction That Works (2nd ed.) by Howard Pitler, Elizabeth R. Hubbell, and Matt Kuhn (#112012)

For up-to-date information about ASCD resources, go to www.ascd.org. You can search the complete archives of *Educational Leadership* at www.ascd.org/el.

ASCD EDge® Group

Exchange ideas and connect with other educators interested in engaged and inspired practice on the social networking site ASCD EDge at http://ascdedge.ascd.org/

ASCD myTeachSource®

Download resources from a professional learning platform with hundreds of research-based best practices and tools for your classroom at http://myteachsource.ascd.org/

For more information, send an e-mail to member@ascd.org; call 1-800-933-2723 or 703-578-9600; send a fax to 703-575-5400; or write to Information Services, ASCD, 1703 N. Beauregard St., Alexandria, VA 22311-1714 USA.